NATURAL
PARENTING

NATURAL
PARENTING

A practical guide for fathers and mothers: conception to age 3

Peter and Fiona Walker

BLOOMSBURY

A GAIA ORIGINAL

Written by Peter and Fiona Walker

Photography by Fausto Dorelli

Pre-birth photography by Lennart Nilsson

Direction:	Lucy Lidell
	Joss Pearson
	Patrick Nugent
Editorial:	Rosanne Hooper
Design:	Sara Mathews
Illustrations:	Peter Mennim
Animal illustrations:	Binny Mathews
Production:	Susan Walby
	David Pearson

First published in Great Britain 1987
Bloomsbury Publishing Ltd,
4 Bloomsbury Place,
London WC1A 2QA

Typesetting by Peter Furtado, Twickenham
Colour reproduction by F.E. Burman Ltd, London
Printed and bound in Great Britain by
Purnell Book Production Limited
Member of the BPCC Group

ISBN: 0 7475 0020 7

By the same author

Baby Gymnastics
Baby Relax
Going for Gold (with Daley Thompson)

Some comments on this book
Dr Charles Edmondson MA MRCP MRCGP
"Peter and Fiona Walker have created a new and exciting book which takes a fresh look at the time from early conception to toddlerhood. It is a uniquely blended account of the delicate anatomical and physiological changes taking place in both mother and baby, with simultaneous suggestions of how to achieve physical and emotional fitness for ourselves and our unborn child. At last fathers are involved in a more positive way, and early parenting is transformed into a unique life experience."

Alice Coyle (Independent midwife and mother)
"A book I'd recommend for the modern nuclear family."

Carol A. Hicks FIST ASA Staff Tutor
"Water awareness cannot start too early. Peter and Fiona Walker's beautifully illustrated book shows parents a safe and enjoyable way to introduce children to the water."

The positions, massage, and exercises illustrated in this book include effective, pleasurable techniques for the mother-to-be during pregnancy and labour, for the baby from the first few months to early childhood, and for the father before and after the birth. All the assisted exercises for pregnancy and infancy are routines to practise together, with care and concern and the full co-operation of the baby or adult involved.

If you have any history of complications during pregnancy or birth, you should consult your physician before attempting any postures or exercises. Childbirth education is essential if you wish to remain responsible for the way you give birth. To complement this book, you are strongly advised to contact a national childbirth organization, such as the Active Birth Centre, the National Childbirth Trust, or the Birth Centre. These groups will supply a wealth of valuable information and support for pregnancy, birth, and early infancy. It is also a good idea to seek the support of a local couples class and to obtain information about breast- and bottle-feeding from the La Leche League.

The adult and baby stretching exercises are designed to enhance flexibility and relaxation throughout the body, but there are a few precautions to be observed. If you notice acute pain, stiffness, numbness, swelling, or discoloration in any muscle or joint, do not exercise, but consult an osteopath, chiropractor, or physiotherapist. Never practise exercises against your baby's will, immediately after a feed, or if he or she shows any sign of fever, illness, or pain. Never take your child swimming or practise upside-down exercises if he or she has an ear or eye infection. And ensure that all young children are supervised near water.

Above all, this book was conceived as a companion to affectionate and pleasurable physical communication – designed to enhance family relationships and to ensure fitness and health right from the start.

The symbols used in the exercises are as follows:
♀ = Woman/mother ♂ = Man/father ☆ = Child

CONTENTS

FOREWORD

By Yehudi Gordon

I am very pleased to write this foreword for Peter and Fiona Walker's book. This is a timely addition to the literature available to prospective parents and those with young children. I agree with both the philosophy of the book and its natural approach to birth and childcare – with the way it assists active birth, free of drugs and medical intervention, and the emphasis it lays on enhancing the physical fitness of mother, father, and child after the birth, through a series of gentle, yoga-based exercises.

The book traces the development of the baby from conception to the age of three. During pregnancy, the accent is on simple stretching for the expectant mother, with relaxing massage given by her partner. Active birth is encouraged through a series of postures in which the man supports the woman in the positions she may need during labour – from lying down to squatting and kneeling. These positions assist labour by enhancing uterine contractions, making use of gravity and improving the flow of blood to the baby, which in turn reduce the need for drugs and intervention during childbirth.

The main strength of the book lies in its treatment of the period after birth. In the early months, communication is largely non-verbal with body contact and touch forming the main link between parent and baby. During these months, the Walkers show how parents can cultivate their relationship with their baby through soft massage and stretching, which stimulate the body and improve relaxation. Gentle yoga-based exercises are included to help both parents to maintain fitness in the years following the arrival of a new baby. After three months, the exercises for pre-toddlers concentrate on flexibility and increase a baby's relaxed strength and self-confidence. From 15 months onward, the exercises are presented in an imaginative way, using animal stories to encourage the child to stand, squat, twist, and bend – an approach which is bound to capture the attention of children of this age who find it difficult to stay still for long. The final chapter on learning to swim adds an element of safety while introducing children to another dynamic activity.

Natural Parenting treats stretching and relaxation as a way of life. All the exercises, apart from swimming, are designed to be done at home, not only catering for the needs of mother, father and baby, but also enhancing the cohesion of the family. Some are to practise alone, others include positional massage for one member of the family to give to another. This form of physical contact is a powerful way of encouraging communication in the family – especially useful with babies before they can talk. Also, the shared activity helps to involve both parents in the experience of birth and childcare.

Peter and Fiona have designed the book as an adjunct to childbirth education and do not set out to analyse the medical problems which occasionally complicate birth and infancy. Instead, they explore, through soft exercise and massage, a way of helping men, women, and children to keep in touch with their own bodies and to stay in touch with each other. Any family who uses this book will find it a reliable foundation for increasing strength, fitness, and flexibility.

Yehudi Gordon   Consultant Obstetrician

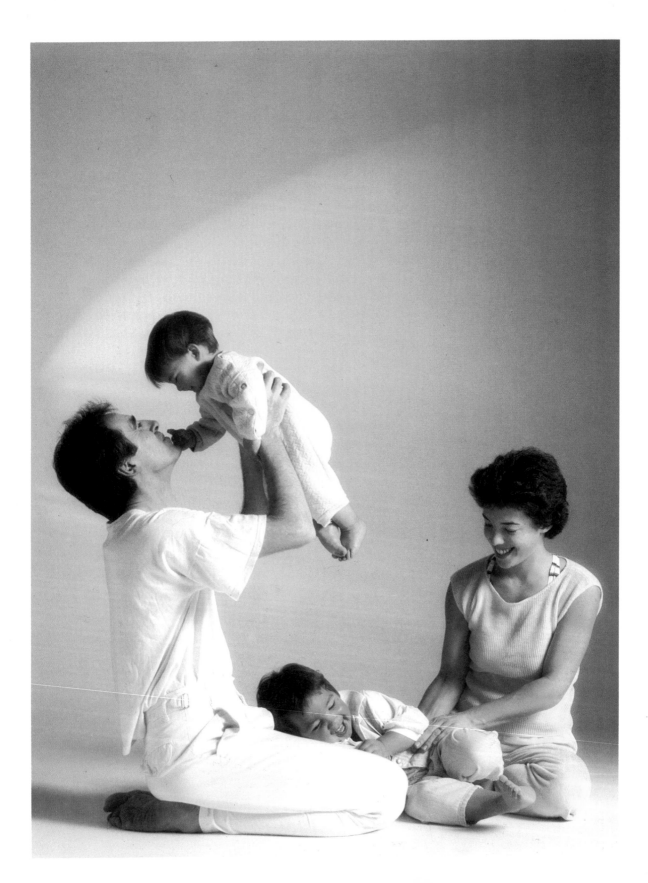

INTRODUCTION

This book evolved from the pleasurable experiences we have shared with our two children, Jason and Mimi. Its main purpose is to encourage those starting a family to improve health and fitness and to develop communication through movement and touch. We also hope to de-mystify some of the important physical aspects of pregnancy, birth, and infancy – and to give new parents, especially fathers, the means to participate fully in the birth and early life of their children.

Pregnancy, birth, and the role of the father

The joy of conception – of creating a unique individual with potential characteristics special to you both – naturally adds a new dimension to your relationship. And by expressing this closeness through increased physical care and attention during pregnancy and birth, the man can help his partner to gain the confidence she needs to take more responsibility for herself and her growing baby. Pregnancy, and the physiological changes that accompany it, offer an ideal opportunity for a woman to improve her wellbeing and so cultivate her body's inherent ability to support the developing child and to give birth.

Birth is the making of a family – and it is an experience that, far from enforcing a period of separation, should bring partners closer together. Emotional anxiety is known to affect the progress of labour, and the presence of a loving, competent companion not only reassures the woman, but can help to minimize external disruptions. This may be even more necessary if she is not giving birth in her own familiar surroundings, and feels less free to move around as she wishes. Birth is likely to be an intense experience, but it will be made all the more manageable by physical preparation and by adopting the right position. Some of the positions recommended to prepare the body for birth can also be effective during labour.

A strong companion who physically supports the woman during labour can help her to give birth in the way that she finds most natural. Among the inhabitants of the Hawaiian Islands, it was reported that women gave birth supported from behind by their partners. These women remained active during labour and instinctively adopted the easiest position for giving birth – usually an upright one. This approach, still practised in parts of Africa and Asia, explains why women from traditional societies generally appear to have more positive, satisfying births than their more sophisticated contemporaries.

Throughout history, the position of women in society has symbolized the level of civilization that society has achieved – a point reflected clearly in the treatment of women during childbirth. In the golden age of Rome, for example, Soranus Ephesus introduced childbirth techniques based on gentle treatment and sensible rational care, instead of on superstition – an attitude that unfortunately lost credibility during the Middle Ages and did not reappear until the Renaissance some 1400 years later. Undoubtedly, recent advances in modern medicine have vastly reduced the fears and risks associated with a complicated delivery. But with an uncomplicated birth, if the woman is well informed and well prepared, and if she can rely on both the skill and co-operation of the midwife and the reassurance of a considerate companion, she can expect the birth to be a unique and rewarding experience for herself and her partner.

The needs of the newborn baby
After birth, close physical contact is essential to reassure the new baby that the comforts and security received in the womb will continue. The experience of birth, although demanding on the mother, must be even more so for the baby who is pushed and squeezed through the birth canal and arrives in the world completely defenceless. Weighing, washing, dressing and so on can all wait until the baby is ready. What he or she needs most is the immediate warmth and comfort of the mother, and a sensitive and calm response from everyone present.

Breastfeeding gives the new baby a wonderful start, with both physical and emotional benefits. Perfectly adjusted to the physiological development of the baby's digestive system, breast milk provides both nourishment and immunity to infection. If breastfeeding is not possible, or if complications have arisen during birth, the newborn baby is even more likely to need close physical contact with his or her mother. Of all the senses, touch is the baby's primary form of communication. The first sense to develop, touch brings objects to life, it gives them substance and reality and arouses feeling. To "lose touch" or to be "out of touch" implies an absence of reality or a fundamental lack of understanding. Touch is also an instinctive response – all mammals touch their newborn, usually by licking them from head to tail, for some time after birth.

During these early months is the best time to introduce baby massage, before the baby becomes more active. Both partners can begin with a simple routine to get used to the feel of the new baby, and then develop a more intuitive, spontaneous approach. This kind of physical contact inspires trust and promotes co-ordination and relaxation in all the major muscles of the body. Before long, the young baby begins to stretch out his or her limbs, slowly co-ordinating and strengthening the muscles, and developing flexibility in the joints.

Health, fitness and affection for babies and young children

From about three months, having gained a reasonable degree of head movement and strength in the arms and shoulders, the baby is ready to engage in more active forms of play and communication. Introduced at this time, soft gymnastics, a series of simple flexibility exercises, can form a basis for affectionate games which are as fun as they are beneficial. Among traditional societies babies and young children sleep alongside their mothers, and because they are kept in continuous physical contact, they rarely cry for attention. They are often massaged from birth, held in positions that foster their rapid development, and praised for their physical achievements. Once your child is mobile, affectionate games that complement development will help to fulfil the need for contact and movement and promote wellbeing.

Swimming is an equally beneficial activity that gives children enormous pleasure, while strengthening the heart and lungs. Among the ancient Greeks and Romans, swimming was one of the very first things children were taught. All these kinds of activity – massage, movement, and learning to swim – together help to cultivate a trusting relationship, while giving the father the opportunity to share more equally and actively in the upbringing of his children.

Staying youthful through exercise

Last, but by no means least, the state of health and fitness of both parents is likely to have a profound influence on the extent to which they enjoy their children. Beyond adolescence, there is no further physical development without effort, and if the body is not to decline with age, it needs some form of regular exercise. Soft gymnastic exercises are the easiest and most effective way of restoring the body's natural relaxation and flexibility – and the most convenient, since they can be performed in your own time and in your own home. Practised regularly and with pleasure, the exercises illustrated in this book will not only enable you to take more responsibility for your own and your children's physical wellbeing, but can also enhance your natural talent for expressing physical affection.

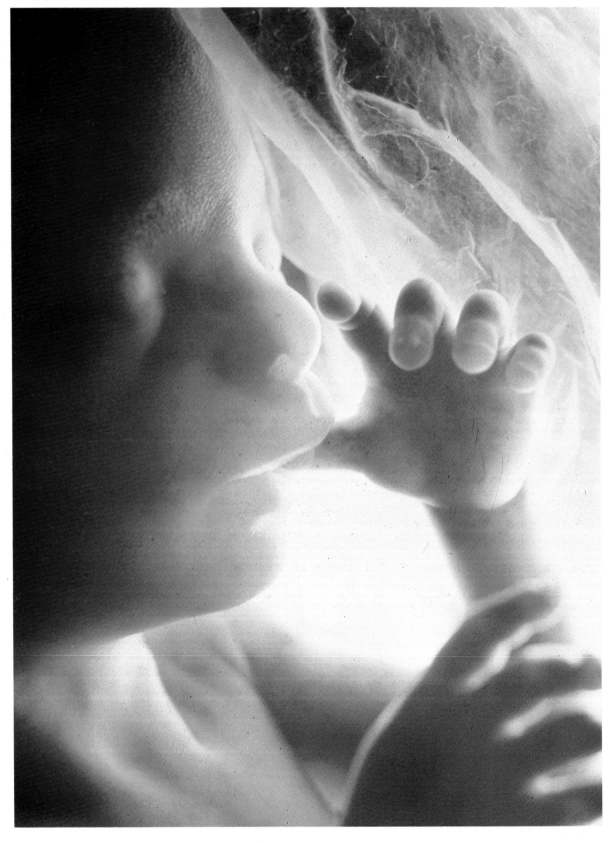

1
LIFE IN THE WOMB

Even before leaving the womb, your baby is already an aware individual – one who can touch, taste, see, hear, move, feel, and respond. From a single cell at conception, the new organism evolves complex human features within weeks, rapidly developing the essential systems for physical, emotional, and intelligent life. And as the brain's communications network forms, the unborn child gradually becomes more conscious of the soft, warm, watery world of the womb. By about four months, it may be aware of the pounding of the mother's heartbeat, the "shushing" sound of her blood pulsing through her blood vessels, and the rumblings of her digestive organs. By five or six months, the baby may even be aware of its parents talking and playing music in the outside world. Precisely when each sense becomes fully functional is still the subject of research, but we do know that a baby born two months prematurely has the use of them all.

With the development of the senses, the child in the womb becomes more receptive to messages from the mother and, through her, to messages about her world. Certainly, the warmth and security of a loving relationship between the parents and the care a woman takes of her body throughout pregnancy – with regular prenatal checkups, sufficient rest, exercise, and nutritious food – can only have a beneficial effect upon the health of the baby and its mother.

The comforts of the womb are thought to form deep, unconscious patterns that may well influence our behaviour throughout our lives. Pre-dispositions toward specific postures, movements, and sounds are clearly recognizable in infants. The fœtal position, to which many children revert at moments of anxiety and during sleep, elicits feelings of security. Young children in need of reassurance often combine this posture with thumb-sucking, another characteristic observed in the womb. "Shushing" a baby, while rocking it to sleep or to stop it crying, is an instant panacea – just as the sound of waves crashing on the seashore helps to relax the mind in later life. Both recall the sound of blood surging through the mother's body, which a number of researchers believe the unborn child can perceive. Likewise, the most popular drum rhythms are around 80 beats a minute, the same tempo as the mother's heartbeat, a reassuring rhythm which accompanies the baby in the womb from the beginning.

The spark that ignites a new human life emerges from touch – the sensual contact between two loving people, mirrored by the fusion of egg and sperm within. Once formed, the cell divides rapidly and within a month has transformed into a recognizable human embryo. In the first three months, the tiny body evolves the complex foundations for human existence: a beating heart, a brain, and a digestive system. By the seventh month, complete with muscles, a skeleton, and a brain that can make complex connections, the baby is equipped to survive in the world. In the final three months, the baby grows to around 20in (50cm), ready for its transition to the world outside.

A new life forms

In the middle of a woman's menstrual cycle, a ripened egg bursts free from the surface of one of her ovaries and passes into the fallopian tube, signalled by a rise in her body temperature. If you make love one or two days before or after this moment, you may sow the seeds of a new life. After intercourse, hundreds of thousands of sperm swim in search of the egg, staying alive for just two or three days. Only one, the fastest swimmer and the first to touch the egg, is admitted; the rest are repelled and die. In that split second of contact, your child's inherited physical traits as well as its sex are decided. After four day's journey along the fallopian tube, this unique individual reaches the womb and embeds itself in the wall. As its outer cells penetrate the blood vessels in the wall of the womb, the new organism forms a primitive placenta – a home and a source of nourishment for the next nine months.

The first three months

At only one month, a tiny heart is already beating and the basis for a brain and spinal cord is starting to form. Now known as an embryo, meaning bud, the tiny being, still only ⅛in (3mm) long, shows early signs of eyes, ears, arms, and legs. By the sixth week, your unborn baby has begun to develop arms and legs and has more distinct, recognizably human features. Floating in a cushioning sac of amniotic fluid, it receives blood, food, and oxygen from the placenta via the umbilical cord. One vein brings oxygenated blood and nutrients in, and two smaller arteries carry blood with carbon dioxide and other waste products back to the placenta. By now the baby is producing its own blood cells, circulating them with each heartbeat. At two months, the new individual displays all the characteristics found in a fully developed human being, and is called a foetus, meaning fruit. You may have only just discovered that you are to be parents, yet your baby's brain, nerves, and muscles are already developing, and its arms and legs are starting to move spontaneously. But at only an inch (2·5cm) long, it is still too small to make you feel these movements. By the twelfth week, the baby measures 3in (7·5cm) and weighs ¾oz (21g); the sexual organs are already clearly defined, and minuscule fingers and toes are growing nail beds. The eyes and nostrils, however, remain closed. As the smaller muscles start to grow, the baby will curl and straighten its toes and, if you press your abdomen, will squirm away. During the next six weeks, the rate of growth accelerates and your baby doubles in size.

The second three months
At around eighteen weeks, you may feel the first little flutters as the baby turns and kicks. A fine down of soft hair, called "lanugo", covers the little body, which can now grip, suck, and co-ordinate thumb-to-mouth movements, and may occasionally cough and hiccup. A spurt of growth occurs in the fifth month, when the gristly skeleton becomes firmer and more bony; by six months, your child already measures over a foot (36cm) long and weighs 2½lbs (1kg). The baby's brain waves are now reflecting patterns of sight and sound, and may move to the rhythm of your voice. The nostrils now open and the chest muscles start breathing-like motions.

The last three months
From the seventh month, this small individual has every chance of survival in the outside world. The eyelids open, revealing blue irises, and the baby wakes and sleeps at more regular intervals. Although fully formed, however, the new human being is still thin and fragile and unable to suck properly. Over the last few weeks, your baby develops an insulating layer of subcutaneous fat and gains a further 2½lbs (1kg) or so in weight, to reach an average birth weight of 6-9lbs (2·7-4kg). The body is now coated in a protective layer of grease, known as "vernix", which protects and nourishes the skin while the baby is in the amniotic fluid. The child now lies head-down and kicks strongly – both mother and father can feel a kick, the mother as sharp sensations in the ribs. At around 40 weeks, too big for the cramped conditions of the womb, your baby is ready to leave this secure first home and, with your help, emerges into the world.

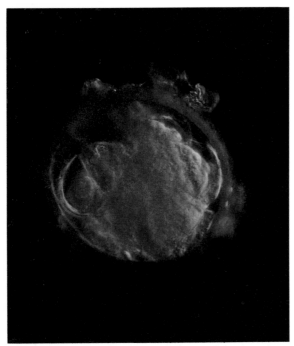

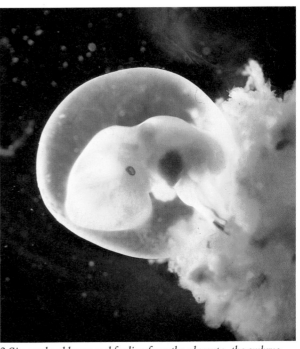

1 An opaque bubble, the fused egg and sperm cell divides and multiplies as it passes along the fallopian tube.

2 Six weeks old now and feeding from the placenta, the embryo displays tiny bud-like arms and legs and a backbone.

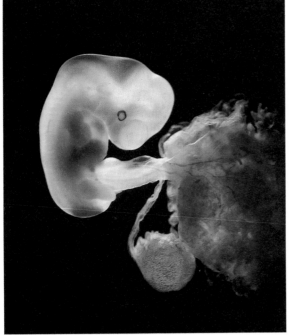

3 Seven weeks old and as the heart pumps up to 50 pints (30 litres) of blood every day, the brain and intestines grow.

4 At around 10 weeks, now looking more human, the ears and eyes and fingers and toes are well formed.

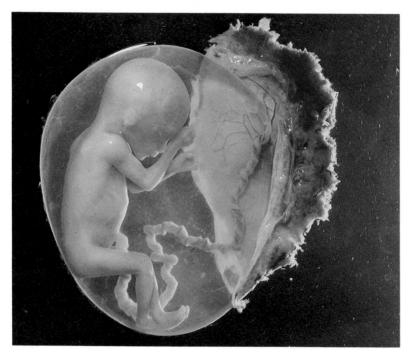

5 Between 12 and 16 weeks, doubling in length, the baby completes its basic development and can co-ordinate movements.

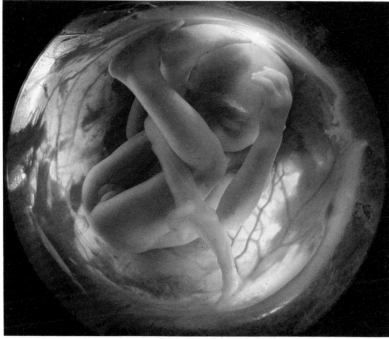

6 At 28 weeks, fully formed and growing fast within its sac of fluid, the baby starts to lay down a store of fat, ready for birth.

A calendar of growth
Week 1
Sperm and egg fuse into a single cell. Passing through the fallopian tube, the organism embeds itself in the wall of the womb.

Week 4   (⅛in – 3mm)
The embryo has the basis of a heart, brain, and nervous system.

Week 6   (¼in – 6mm)
The head and tiny arms and legs begin to take shape, and, as the digestive system develops, the placenta starts to form.

Week 8   (1in – 2·5cm)
The brain, nervous system, and muscles become active.

Week 10   (1¾in – 4·5cm)
The eyes are forming and webbed fingers and toes emerge.

Week 12   (3in – 7·5 cm)
The sex of the baby is now evident and, as the muscles develop, movement increases.

Week 16   (6in – 15cm)
Fed by the placenta, the baby puts on a spurt of growth and becomes more energetic.

Week 18   (7in – 18cm)
Fine down covers the body and bone begins to replace cartilage.

Week 20   (10in – 25cm)
Hair starts to grow on the head.

Week 24   (14in – 35cm)
The nostrils open, and the baby may suck its thumb and hiccup.

Week 28   (15in – 38cm)
Grease covers the skin, and the brain becomes more complex.

Week 32   (16in – 40cm)
The baby is now completely formed, and the lungs are ready to function.

Week 36   (18in – 46cm)
The baby becomes plumper and even grows finger- and toe-nails.

Week 40   (20in – 50cm)
The baby is ready to be born.

THE SENSES

Sounds, tastes, and textures enrich our lives even before we are born. Only our sense of smell remains dormant until the first intake of breath completes our sensory spectrum. The physical foundations for sensory perception begin to emerge from as early as the sixth week in the womb. But it is not until the last three months that a baby evolves the complex mental mechanisms that can translate physical reflexes into sensory and emotional experiences.

The sense of touch

Touch is the first of the senses to develop. At less than nine weeks old, the embryo is thought to respond to light stroking with a reflex movement. As the baby grows larger, and fits more tightly against the protective wall of the abdomen, it may well express a dislike of being poked and prodded with a few well-placed kicks. Once the pregnancy has advanced a little, it is common for the mother to communicate with her baby by instinctively stroking her abdomen in a gentle message of reassurance. The father-to-be may enjoy sharing this gesture too, when appropriate, gently massaging the baby through his partner's abdomen. And you may both feel this contact brings you more in touch with your child.

The sense of hearing

The most pervasive stimulus for the unborn child is sound. The outer ear, auditory canal, and eardrum begin to develop before the sixth week, and by the fifth month, the ears and hearing mechanism are almost complete. At around twenty-four weeks, your baby may already be aware of a constant barrage of noises passing through the amniotic fluid, which conducts sound better than air. The loudest sound is the reassuring boom of the mother's heart, beating in rhythm to the loud "whooshing" sound of blood flowing through the blood vessels. The rumblings of stomach and intestines are no secret to the unborn child, and by the time the woman is six months pregnant, it can hear her voice. Even external sounds – loud voices on the radio and television and talking in the room – are audible inside the womb. Once born, your new baby may recognize not only its mother's voice, but also its father's deeper tones or the chatter of its brothers and sisters. It may even respond to pieces of music you played during pregnancy. According to research, the unborn baby even appears to prefer single-note music, such as flute or guitar solos, to more complex arrangements like rock or classical concertos. A sudden loud bang, such as a door slamming or a car hooting, can make your baby jump – it may deliver a kick in the ribs or turn around, in reply. By the same token, the baby in the womb appears to appreciate the same soft and calming sounds that help you both to relax.

The sense of taste

During the fourth week, the mouth and gastro-intestinal tract begin to form. At four months, the fœtus is swallowing amniotic fluid and passing waste products into its intestinal tract; at five months it is already capable of sucking responses; but its taste buds don't finally develop until around seven months. Even at this stage, a baby appears to like sweet tastes and although it cannot directly taste the nutrients supplied via its mother's bloodstream, it is susceptible to any toxins passed through the placenta.

The sense of sight

In the protective darkness of the womb, a baby has little visual stimulus, yet from an early age it is sensitive to light. At the end of the first month in the womb, the eyes emerge as large, indented ovals, and when the retina develops at five weeks, they become dark circles. At two months, the irises and pupils become visible and the eyelids form. By the twelfth week, the eyelids start to fuse together and although they remain closed until the seventh month, they do admit bright light. At about sixteen weeks, if you are out in the sun, your baby may also feel bathed in light, and if you shine a bright light directly on to the abdomen, you may disturb your tiny offspring. In the month before birth, the baby opens its eyes and gazes abstractedly around. At this stage the abdominal wall has stretched further, allowing natural light to penetrate and become diffused in the fluid, so that the baby may see a glow similar to that seen through a hand held over a torch light. By the time you meet face to face in the outside world, your baby can see well enough to distinguish the contours of your face.

From reflex to emotion

In the first few months, the unborn child appears to feel simple sensations as physical reflexes, but these may become real emotions as soon as the brain begins to translate sensory messages into meaningful experiences during the sixth month in the womb. By the time your baby is ready to be born, it is equipped to respond to your emotions, and to learn from new experiences.

Exploring through touch

Searching fingers reach out and touch from as early as the second month. First they feel the soft texture of the watery surround, then the glossy surface of the skin. After birth, the fingers will express emotions as well as receiving sensations.

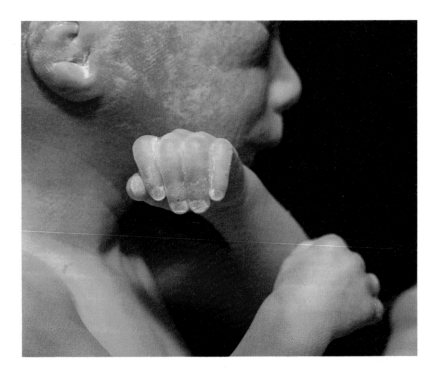

Learning to listen

Fully orchestrated, with a rhythmic heart "boom", a percussive "shush" of blood, and incidental stomach rumblings, the womb is far from silent. The baby begins to be aware of these sounds when the brain starts to interpret sensory patterns at around six months and can detect a change in tempo.

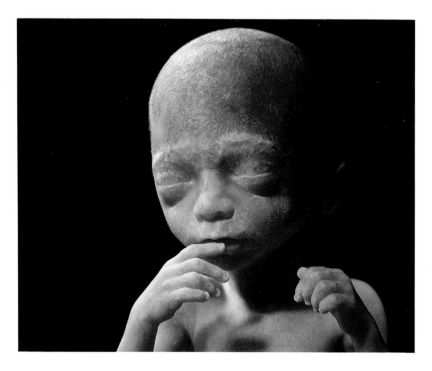

Tasting – a future pleasure

Our first taste is the neutral flavour of amniotic fluid. Sensitive to the slightest change in its sweetness or acidity in rare circumstances, by the seventh month the taste buds are well prepared to savour the first sweet drop of milk after birth.

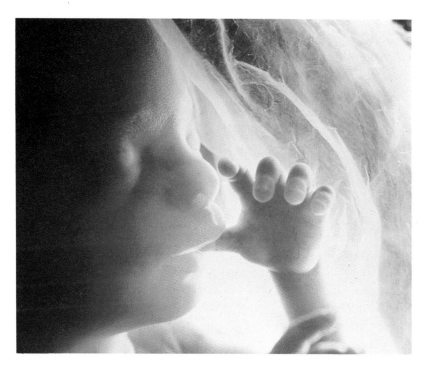

Watching and waiting

Research has shown that the sudden intrusion of bright light into the calm darkness of the womb will penetrate a baby's consciousness, even through closed eyelids. Taken unawares in this way, an infant may instinctively resort to thumb sucking. When the eyelids open in the final month, the eyes can distinguish shapes at close range, so that, by birth, the baby can see the details of its mother's face from less than a foot (30cm) away.

S T A R T   R I G H T

A unique being with its own destiny, your baby's health is none-theless enhanced by the caring attitude you both show as parents in the fragile period of prenatal life. Looking after your own health and happiness in these formative months will in turn benefit your baby, giving it the best possible start in life.

The bond between mother and baby

Nourished by your blood, your baby is bound to you in the closest possible way. Your heart, a life-giving source of vitality and emotion, conveys everything needed to sustain life. Yet the quality of the baby's present and future existence can be significantly influenced by the care you take of yourself during pregnancy.

Throughout pregnancy, periods of rest and silent introspection help to relax your body and mind. Given peace and quiet, many women find themselves naturally "switching off" at around the same time every day. Others, who may be under pressure of time, can initiate this sense of relaxed detachment at convenient moments, by putting aside 10-20 minutes a day, free from disturbance, stress and strain. An ideal way to rest is to sit comfortably in a warm, quiet room, and to allow your breathing to become slower and deeper, descending into your abdomen, as your eyes, face, neck and shoulders relax. This relieves your body of accumulated tension, helps to free your mind from anxieties, and encourages a beneficial state of calm.

Dual responsibility

Physically, you can give your baby a healthy start in life by eating a good balance of fresh, natural foods and keeping salt, sugar, coffee, fàt and refined foods to a minimum. Ideally, your diet should be rich in iron, fibre and vitamin C, and consist of about one third of wholegrain bread, pasta, rice and so on, one third of washed fresh fruit and vegetables, a quarter of lean poultry, fish, nuts, seeds and beans and just a little fat, such as olive oil, margarine and peanut butter.

As a gesture of consideration to your baby and yourself, try to give up smoking, alcohol, drugs, and caffeine in early pregnancy if you have not already done so. Cigarette smoke reaches your baby as carbon monoxide gas, depriving the growing child of oxygen and impeding development. Smokers' babies are known to be smaller than average and are sometimes born prematurely. Alcohol can cause physical abnormalities and impair a child's intelligence. Chemical drugs may also cross the placenta and interfere with your baby's development. Stimulants and depressants play havoc with a baby's nervous system; addictive drugs can produce an addicted child; others cause even greater damage. A further safety measure would be to avoid contact with anyone who has German measles (rubella), if you have not already had the disease or been inoculated against it, especially during the first three months, while the organs are developing.

On the subject of prenatal tests, medical opinion remains divided. The safety of the ultrasound scan, for example, used to detect the size and position of the baby in the womb, is now being questioned by some researchers. And amniocentesis, a test often offered to women in their late thirties and those with a family history of Down's syndrome or other conditions, may upset the delicate tissues in the womb. It is therefore worth considering and discussing the advantages and disadvantages of these tests before agreeing to them.

Your role as father-to-be
Most of us become anxious when we lose touch with the people or things we depend on – especially our partners. This can all too easily happen during pregnancy when as an expectant father you may feel excluded, and unconnected with the tiny individual you have helped to create. The more you understand the changes taking place in your partner, the more involved you will feel.

According to ancient belief, the unborn baby is surrounded by a circle of sympathetic magic, in the nine months or so before birth. Among more "primitive" cultures, the father-to-be is expected to fast, to eat only certain foods, to curb any violent behaviour during pregnancy and to practise rituals that evoke the same intensity of sensation as that experienced by the woman in labour.

In our own culture, a man can express his enthusiasm by sharing as much as possible in his partner's experience. It is only natural for her to become emotionally overwhelmed from time to time, to be depressed, moody, irritable, or tearful, to fear for the normality of her child and for her own capacity to give birth and adequately fulfil her role as a mother. A little sympathetic understanding from you will do much to allay her doubts and fears and help to restore her emotional equilibrium. As your baby develops, you will find that your partner's focus of attention slowly shifts from external events to the interaction taking place within. Recognizing her quiet periods of introspection, giving her space, and protecting her from disruptive influences are all vital aspects of being a good father.

2
SHARING PREGNANCY

A woman's feelings toward her own pregnancy and the attitude of those closest to her can greatly influence the ease with which she carries her child. The sense of anticipation and joy that accompanies pregnancy is inevitably punctuated by times of uncertainty, physical discomfort, and tiredness. It is at such moments that a loving and supportive partner can make all the difference.

In Western society, the father's role in pregnancy has long been undervalued, even considered an optional extra, but if he feels involved, a man can provide a wealth of practical and emotional assistance. This can be as rewarding as finding out about the growth of the baby and learning exercises, as supportive as listening to a woman's worries and soothing her aches and pains, and as simple as sharing the chores and encouraging her to rest. Having a child, after all, is a family affair, and the more a man participates in these early days, the closer he will feel to both mother and baby in the years to come.

A man's moral and physical support can be particularly helpful when a woman starts to actively prepare her body for the birth. Gently massaging her while she exercises can transform her activity into a pleasurable, shared experience. Exercises are an invaluable means of maintaining physical wellbeing throughout pregnancy and birth; they alleviate stress and strain and can condition the body to respond with greater ease to the demands of labour. Stretching exercises are especially beneficial; they become more effective when hormonal changes during pregnancy soften the muscles of the pelvis, allowing them to stretch and relax more easily.

This chapter offers two complementary exercise routines: Relax is a series of partner-assisted sequences, which gradually build up during each term of pregnancy until they include all the muscles and joints that engage in childbirth. Stretch is a self-help routine, introduced in the second term, for the woman to practise alone. Both these programmes, if practised regularly, are an effective and enjoyable preparation for birth. Of all these exercises, learning to relax the pelvic floor to prevent the muscles tearing during childbirth is the most important. Making love also helps a woman to stay in touch with these muscles, and provided the emphasis is on loving care, it can enhance the sensual pleasure of pregnancy.

R E L A X

Relieving tension in pregnancy

Pregnancy spans about 40 weeks and is divided into three "terms" of three months. Each term places different physical and emotional demands on a woman. During the first term the woman may find her mood erratic while adjusting to motherhood. In the second term, as the placenta produces hormones of its own, nausea and fatigue are often replaced by a feeling of self-confidence and a glow of good health. In the third term, the mother may begin to need more rest and relaxation as the baby grows heavier. In this section we give a progressive series of exercises designed specifically to help you both to relax generally, and to maintain a relaxed tone in the woman's postural muscles (see pp. 140-1). Throughout pregnancy, gently massaging the abdomen with an oil rich in vitamin E can be very soothing and may help to minimize stretch marks.

TERM ONE

Positional massage for weeks 1-12

Rest, relaxation, and freedom from emotional stress are all important in early pregnancy. Practising Abdominal breathing exercises together will relax you both, improve your respiration, circulation, and digestion and help to relieve any slight dizziness and nausea a woman may feel. It also gives you both an opportunity to spend a few quiet minutes together every day and to turn your attention inward. Massage of the head and neck, a common site of emotional tension, brings a sense of relief to neck and shoulder muscles that is felt throughout the body. Massage of the feet and calf muscles at this stage is relaxing generally, and improves circulation throughout pregnancy. Try to practise this whole sequence for half an hour, two or three times a week, including five or ten minutes of breathing exercises.

Abdominal breathing

Breathing naturally and slowly through the abdomen cultivates a state of calm relaxation. It allows your body to consume a lot of air for a little effort.

♂ *Sit comfortably behind your partner and place your hands between her lower ribs and navel. On the out-breath, press gently.*
♀ *Kneeling, breathe in through your nostrils and out through your mouth, slowly and evenly. Focus your attention on the rise and fall of your navel, watching it draw in as you breathe out.*

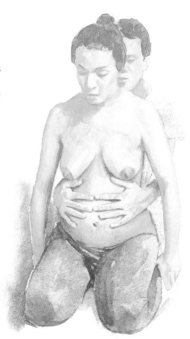

Your anatomy in the first term

During the first three months, you will notice very little visible change. Pressure on your bladder may make you want to pass water more frequently.

Feet, ankles, and calves

Your lower legs and feet bear the full weight of the body. Any cramp or strain here can affect its entire structural balance. A little positional massage now will improve your circulation, prevent cramps, and help relaxation.

1♀ Lie comfortably on a sofa with one foot in your partner's lap.
♂ Extend the heel by pushing on the upper part of the foot and turning it outward from below the toes. Knead the calf muscles from below the back of the knee down to the heel, using your whole hand.

2 ♂ Press your fingers and thumb around the achilles tendon and massage gently all around the back and sides of the heel bone.

3 ♂ Turn the foot inward, pressing the ball of the big toe as you rotate it inward with your fingers.

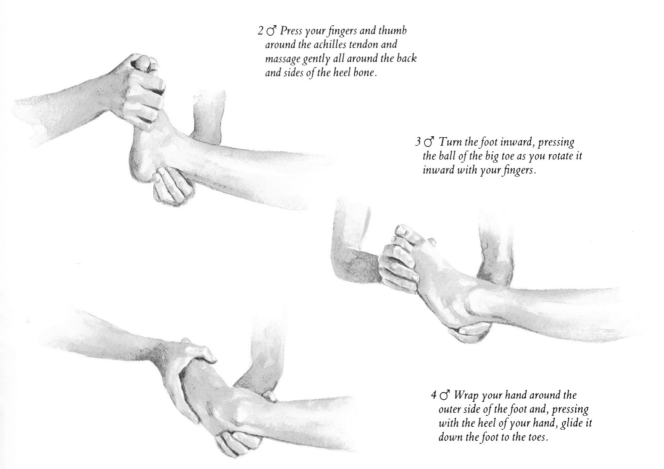

4 ♂ Wrap your hand around the outer side of the foot and, pressing with the heel of your hand, glide it down the foot to the toes.

5 ♂ Roll and pull each toe with your thumb and forefinger, then spread the toes by gently pulling them in opposite directions.

6 ♂ Press your fingers into the front of the ankle joint and massage the area gently.

7 ♂ Using the pressure of your thumb and forefingers, feel and massage the lower joint of each toe.

8 ♂ Flex the toes with one hand and massage the centre of the sole of the foot with the fingers of your other hand. Then massage all around the bony arch of the foot.

9 ♀ Face the wall, stretch your arms up and bend your left knee against the wall. Step back with your right foot and put your heel to the floor. Relax your shoulders.
♂ Gently stroke down the length of the calf muscle, using your whole hand. Repeat on the other side.

Head and neck

The neck carries the head and all the main channels of life support. Extremely vulnerable, the neck muscles shorten in response to cold weather, emotional anxiety, and shock and adjust their tension to changes in posture. A massage to relax these muscles usually prevents and eases pains in the head, neck and shoulders, and relieves tension.

1 ♀ Lie on your back with a cushion under your knees to straighten your lower spine. Pull your shoulder-blades together, then relax.
♂ Sit comfortably cross-legged on the edge of a cushion, with your partner's head in your lap. Spread your hands around her head above the ears and gently pull and release in a rocking motion.

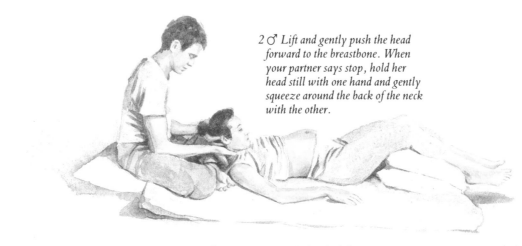

2 ♂ Lift and gently push the head forward to the breastbone. When your partner says stop, hold her head still with one hand and gently squeeze around the back of the neck with the other.

3 ♂ Still supporting the head, slide your other hand down the upper back as far as you can. Gently press and release the muscles on each side of the spine, slowly working up to the top of the neck.

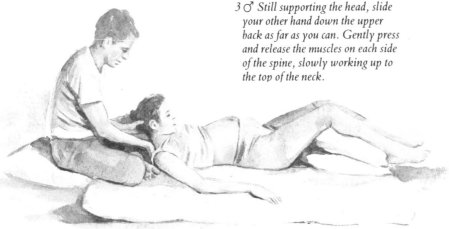

Caution:
If you feel dizzy at any point, stop immediately, and rest.

4 ♂ *Keep the head lifted, the chin slightly tucked in and, using both hands, gently move the left ear to the left shoulder. When the right shoulder begins to lift, rest the head on your calf and hold it in place with one hand. Use the other hand to gently squeeze the right side of the neck. Repeat on both sides.*

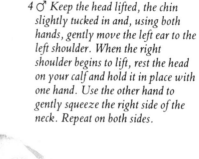

5 ♂ *Keep the chin slightly tucked in and, crossing your hands, put your right hand above the left ear and your left hand above the right ear. Rotate the head to the left, as far as it will go, rest it on your leg and hold the position for 30 seconds.*

6 ♂ *Holding the head in position with your right hand, massage the neck with your left hand. Repeat both exercises on the right side.*

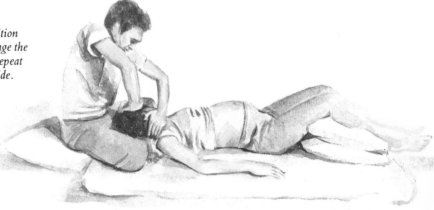

TERM TWO

Positional massage for weeks 13-24

Walking in the fresh air and swimming together will improve your health and fitness at this time. Swimming is especially helpful, because it promotes suppleness and flexibility, while the water supports your weight. Follow up your Abdominal breathing now with Upper abdominal breathing – a slightly higher and faster breath – for five minutes a day. As the baby's weight increases in mid-pregnancy, regular massage of the woman's postural muscles – the legs and buttocks – (see pp.140-1) can prevent and relieve aches, pains and general tiredness. Continue your term one exercises and combine them with the following sequence, taking about an hour, two or three times a week. If you find yourself short of time, try at least to practise pelvic floor exercises every week.

Upper abdominal breathing

This technique will allow you to breathe rhythmically when you are in the grip of a contraction. If you practise this now, it will come naturally during labour.

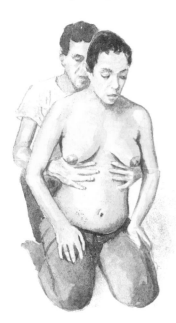

♂ *Kneel comfortably behind your partner and place your hands around the sides of her lower ribcage. Do not press.*
♀ *Kneeling, breathe in through your nostrils and out through your mouth, more quickly than normal. If you feel dizzy, slow down the rhythm.*

Your anatomy in the second term

♀ As the womb expands, the extra weight will put a strain on your lower back and legs, and increased pressure on your stomach and intestines may give you indigestion.

Thighs, buttocks and pelvic floor

The thighs and buttocks work hard to support the increasing weight of the baby. Some of these postural muscles lead into the pelvic floor (see pp. 140-1), where five main muscle groups converge. These exercises soften and relax the pelvic area for birth and relieve fatigue. They continue overleaf.

1 ♀ *Lie on your side with your knees bent and one leg overlapping the other. Relax, and breathe deeply.*
♂ *Kneel behind your partner. Using the fingertips or heel of one hand, press firmly around the sides of her sacrum at the base of her spine and follow it upward around the inside of the hip wing. Work inward around the buttocks with a circular, kneading motion.*

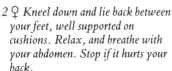

2 ♀ *Kneel down and lie back between your feet, well supported on cushions. Relax, and breathe with your abdomen. Stop if it hurts your back.*
♂ *Massage the front of both thighs, kneading with your whole hand from the knee to the hip bone.*

3 ♀ *Squat with your knees open. Put your arms around your partner's neck, relax, and breathe with your abdomen. Contract and relax your pelvic floor, by tensing your vaginal and anal muscles as if you are trying not to pass water.*
♂ *Kneel or sit on a chair to support your partner and gently knead the sides of her arms and ribcage.*

4 ♀ *Sit with the soles of your feet together and your knees open, and hold on to your feet. Relax, and breathe with your abdomen. Contract and relax your pelvic floor four or five times.*
♂ *Sitting behind your partner, place the balls of your feet under the bony wings of her hips. Push and lift gently but firmly.*

5 ♀ *Sit on your feet with your knees spread wide, and lean forward on to a pile of cushions. Relax, and breathe with your abdomen. Contract and relax your pelvic floor four or five times.*
♂ *Using a little oil or powder, massage down each side of her spine with your fingertips. Work down to the buttocks three or four times.*

6 ♀ *Stay in the same position and contract and relax your pelvic floor four or five times.*
♂ *Lean slowly forward as you massage smoothly but firmly around the two dimples at the base of her spine and around her buttocks.*

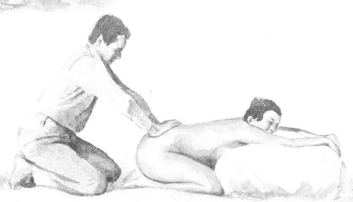

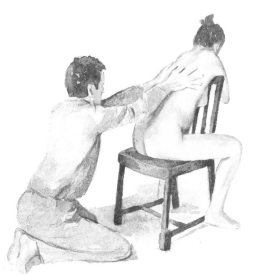

7 ♀ *Sit astride a chair and lean forward with a straight spine. Keeping your knees wide open and both feet pressed to the ground, contract and relax your pelvic floor four or five times.*
♂ *Using a little oil or powder, spread your hands and glide your thumbs up and down either side of her spine three or four times.*

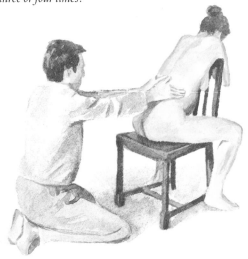

8 ♀ *Stay in the same position.*
♂ *Using the heels of both hands, lean forward and massage her buttocks, with a slow but firm circular motion.*

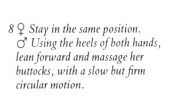

TERM THREE

Positional massage for weeks 25-40

Loose, comfortable clothes, flat shoes, plenty of rest and relaxation and eating little and often help to make the last months easier. Include Light breathing exercises now after your Abdominal and Upper abdominal breathing, keeping your body relaxed throughout. As the baby gains weight, it tends to pull the shoulders and upper back forward, compressing the abdominal organs and diaphragm. Positional massage of the back and shoulders helps to keep the spine strong and straight and the chest and shoulders open, which in turn helps to ease digestion and breathing. Continue your term one and term two exercises, and follow them up now with this sequence for the upper body, two or three times a week. Make a special effort to concentrate on your pelvic floor exercises, particularly in the lead-up to birth.

Light breathing

Shallow breathing, associated with strenuous activity, will be useful in the later stages of labour. By reducing the movement of the abdominal muscles, it will help you to delay pushing your baby out before the cervix is fully opened.

♂ *Kneel comfortably behind your partner and place your hands across her upper chest.*
♀ *Kneel and breathe quite rapidly in through your nostrils and out through your mouth for one or two minutes, with your mouth relaxed. Focus on your ribcage as it rises and falls just below your shoulders. Slow the rhythm right down if you feel dizzy.*

Your anatomy in the third term

♀ As the top of the womb rises to the breastbone and presses against the lungs, you may feel breathless. At around 36 weeks, the baby's head engages in the pelvic cavity, ready for birth.

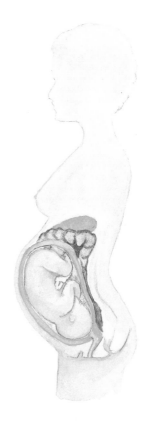

Spine, back and shoulders

The body is as strong as the spine that supports it. If the lower back and shoulder muscles lose their strength, the forward pull of the expanding abdomen will move the body's centre of gravity. This puts extra strain on the postural muscles and, through them, on the pelvic floor. By maintaining the integrity of the spinal column, the following exercises in turn help the pelvic floor, chest and abdomen to remain relaxed.

1 ♀ Go down on all fours, then lower your weight forward with your buttocks raised, your forehead resting on the floor, and your arms extended straight forward. Relax, and breathe with your abdomen.
♂ Kneel in front of your partner. Using your whole hand, gently massage the sides of her arms and shoulders with smooth strokes.

2 ♀ Stay in the same position.
♂ Place your hands at the base of her arms and gently massage the sides of her arms and chest.

3 ♀ Stay in the same position.
♂ Place your hands on each shoulder-blade and, using a little body weight, push slowly and firmly back down the centre of her spine, then release. Repeat three or four times.

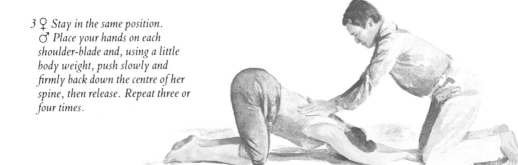

4 ♀ *Kneel down and sit back on your feet with your back straight. Stretch your arms up and interlock your fingers. Breathe with your abdomen.*
♂ *Kneel behind your partner (left) – or sit on a chair (right) – with her hands around your neck. Massage the sides of her upper arms and straighten her arms by slowly lifting upward. Encourage your partner to relax her shoulders, adjusting your hold immediately.*

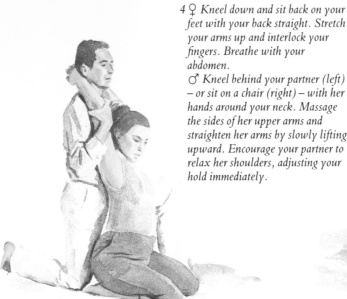

5 ♀ *Sit comfortably cross-legged, or kneel and sit back with your back against a chair. Relax and breathe with your abdomen.*
♂ *Sit on a chair behind your partner and, using your fingers and thumbs, massage from the base of the neck right along to the tips of the shoulder-blades.*

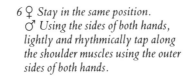

6 ♀ *Stay in the same position.*
♂ *Using the sides of both hands, lightly and rhythmically tap along the shoulder muscles using the outer sides of both hands.*

Caution:
♀ If you feel dizzy or in pain at any moment, stop immediately. Guide your partner, so that he knows exactly where and how hard to press at each stage.

S T R E T C H

Solo exercises for Terms Two and Three

♀Giving birth will be easier and more pleasurable if you are relaxed, physically well-prepared, and in touch with your own body. All the major muscles and joints need to be supple to adjust to the demands of childbirth, but it is the abdominal and pelvic muscles and the pelvic joints that undergo the most extreme expansion and contraction. The following exercises and the breast care routine, both specifically designed to help you prepare yourself for the birth, also allow you to centre yourself both mentally and physically. You will find them most effective if you practise Abdominal breathing (see p.29) and, where possible, if you massage the area you are exercising. Practise this sequence quietly alone for about an hour, two or three times a week. After each exercise, relax and take four or five abdominal breaths before continuing.

Stretching the lower back and pelvis

1 Assume an all-fours position. Relax your neck and shoulders and breathe with your abdomen.

2 Tuck in your pelvis and make several wide clockwise movements with your hips. Keep your shoulders relaxed, and breathe with your abdomen. Repeat counter-clockwise.

Strengthening the shoulders

3 Lean forward with your arms straight ahead and rest your forehead on the floor. Try to push your breastbone forward. Relax, and breathe with your abdomen.

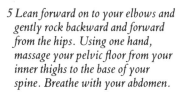

Stretching the pelvic floor

4 Rest forward on to your hands and open your knees wide. Relax your shoulders and breathe with your abdomen. Contract and relax your pelvic floor ten times.

5 Lean forward on to your elbows and gently rock backward and forward from the hips. Using one hand, massage your pelvic floor from your inner thighs to the base of your spine. Breathe with your abdomen.

Opening the shoulders and relaxing the lower back

6 Lie on your back and lift your knees. Extend your left arm in line with your left shoulder and twist your legs and hips to the right. Hold your knees down with your right hand. Relax, and repeat on the other side.

Stretching the pelvic floor

7 Sit upright on the edge of a cushion, supported if necessary against a wall. Bring the soles of your feet together and open your knees. Contract and relax your pelvic floor and buttocks about 12 times. Then push your knees open gently, relax, and breathe with your abdomen.

8 Push down gently on one knee with one hand and massage along your inside thigh to your pelvic floor with the other. Repeat for the other leg. Relax, and breathe with your abdomen.

Stretching the legs and ankles

9 Sit on your feet with your toes turned inward. Relax your shoulders, and breathe with your abdomen.

Strengthening the lower back and stretching the legs and abdomen

10 Lean back on your hands or elbows, tighten your buttocks and push your hips forward. Hold for two or three breaths, but stop if this exercise hurts your back.

Stretching the neck and shoulders

11 Sit on or between your feet, interlock your fingers behind your head, hold your elbows together and let the weight of your arms pull your head forward. Relax, and breathe with your abdomen.

12 Encircle your head with your left arm. Keep your chin slightly tucked in and let your arm pull your ear to your shoulder. Massage your right shoulder with your right hand. Relax, and breathe with your abdomen. Repeat on the other side.

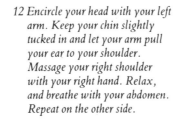

Stretching the pelvic floor

13 Squat with your hands on the floor between your knees. Push your knees open with your elbows. Relax, and breathe. Contract and relax your pelvic floor and massage from inside your thighs back to the base of your spine. Then squat with your feet and heels on the floor and massage your inside thighs back to the base of your spine. Relax.

Stretching the lower back and legs

14 Rest your hands on the back of a stable chair. Lean forward, walk backward, keeping your weight on both feet. Relax your neck, and lift your buttocks.

Stretching the inside thighs

15 Hold the same position and open your legs as wide as is comfortable, keeping your feet turned inward. Relax, and breathe with your abdomen then lift your buttocks. Hold for a minute or two.

Unwinding

16 Relax in your most comfortable position for about 10 minutes. This gives your body a chance to re-adjust after stretching.

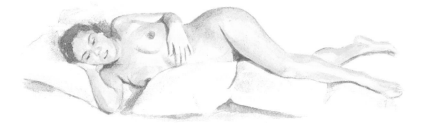

BREAST CARE

Preparing for breastfeeding

♀ Whether you intend to breastfeed or not, breast care during pregnancy can make you feel both more comfortable and more confident. In the early months, as your breasts become larger, heavier, and more sensitive, wear a well-fitting bra that does not flatten your nipples. To keep your nipples in good condition, wash them with warm water and avoid soap, which dries the natural oil secreted by the areola surrounding the nipple. If they do feel tender, apply a little lanolin. During the last term, your nipples may spontaneously secrete a form of milk known as colostrum. Expressing a little colostrum by massaging the breasts can be reassuring. If your nipples are flat or inverted, practise stretching the areola and, if you enjoy it, encourage your partner to include gentle oral stimulation in lovemaking.

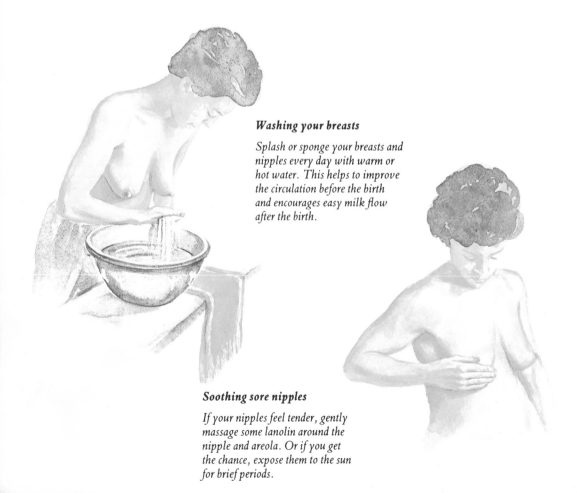

Washing your breasts

Splash or sponge your breasts and nipples every day with warm or hot water. This helps to improve the circulation before the birth and encourages easy milk flow after the birth.

Soothing sore nipples

If your nipples feel tender, gently massage some lanolin around the nipple and areola. Or if you get the chance, expose them to the sun for brief periods.

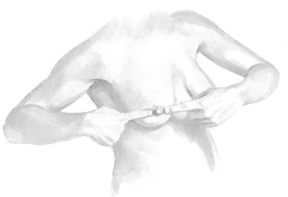

Correcting inverted nipples

1 Place your index fingers on each side of your nipple and stretch the areola by drawing your fingers sideways.

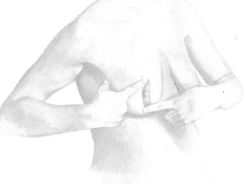

2 Place your index fingers above and below the nipple and stretch the areola vertically. Continue this movement clockwise around the nipple until you have stretched the areola in all directions.

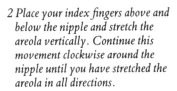

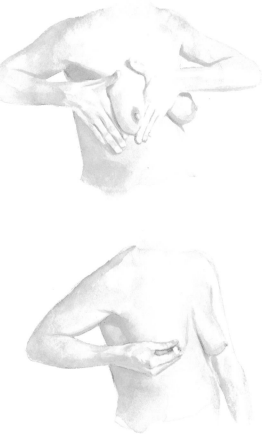

Expressing milk

1 Place both hands flat against your ribcage on both sides of your breast, so that the "V" of your thumb and index finger surrounds each side.

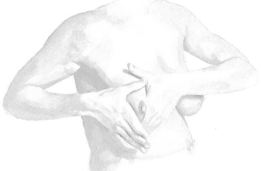

2 With one gentle movement, draw your hands down toward your nipple until your index fingers surround its base.

3 Now gently squeeze the areola with your thumb and forefinger until a drop of milk emerges.

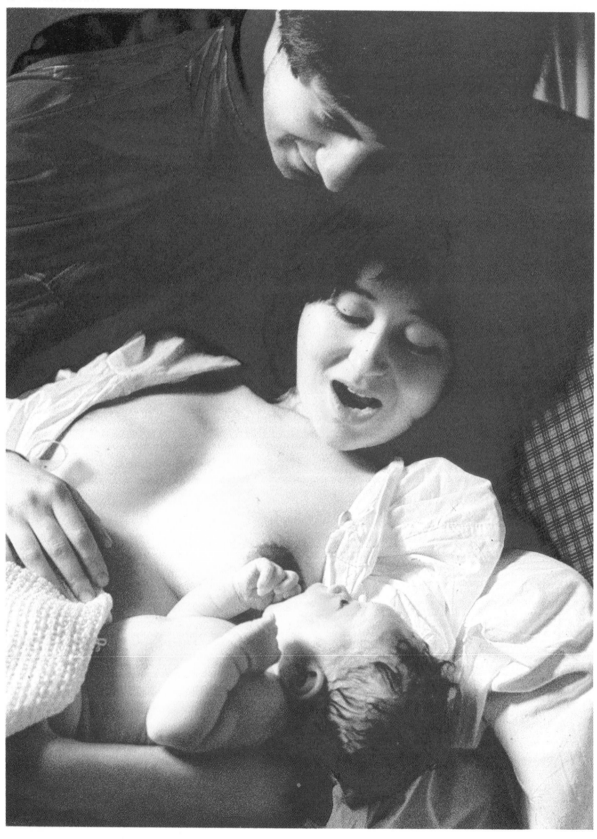

3
GIVING BIRTH

To understand what it takes to give birth and what it means to be born, the man must be present. Sharing the intimacy of labour and witnessing the miraculous moment of birth itself, arouses a whole new depth of feeling and understanding. Everyone who participates in a birth feels closely involved, nobody more so than the expectant father. By encouraging and physically supporting his partner when she most needs it, he deepens his attachment to both mother and baby, and creates a stronger foundation for their future together as a family.

For the woman about to give birth, it is immensely reassuring to know that she can rely on the support of a competent and loving companion. An understanding partner who will respond immediately to her requests, comfort and support her through each stage of labour and mediate with the outside world, leaves her free to concentrate her energies on what is taking place within. Labour is strenuous and demanding, but is undoubtedly less tiring and far more comforting if the woman has someone she is fond of to hold her and to help her co-ordinate her breathing and remain relaxed.

The choice of a home or a hospital birth may be determined as much by health, age, and medical history as by personal preference. But wherever birth takes place, the mother-to-be will feel more relaxed and comfortable if she has some control over the management of her labour. To do this the woman must be free to remain active and to assume positions that she intuitively finds the most comfortable during labour and birth. In order to ensure this freedom, the parents-to-be will need the co-operation of the hospital or community midwife well before birth, and in the case of a hospital birth, this agreement should be recorded. Both parents would be well advised to gain a full understanding of birth and obstetric practices, from national childbirth organizations and local couples classes.

This chapter shows how the man can support his partner in the most comfortable positions for each stage of labour and birth. By using the power of gravity and allowing the pelvic muscles to stretch and the pelvic joints to open more easily, the positions in this chapter aid the descent of the baby. When combined with rhythmic breathing and, if needed, some gentle massage, these positions create the best possible conditions for the woman to give birth in her own natural way.

THE BABY'S POSITION

How the baby "presents" itself for birth

♀In the last few weeks of pregnancy, your baby's head descends into the lower part of your womb, ready for birth. Variations in presentation are common, but most babies lie head-down, facing half-back toward your spine, so that one ear lines up with your navel. Known as "anterior presentation", this is generally considered the easiest position for birth. Some babies lie head-down, facing the front of the abdomen. Known as "posterior presentation", this can mean a slower labour with more back pain but the baby will usually turn its head just before birth. Occasionally, a baby lies head uppermost, in the "breech" position, so that the head is delivered last, after the umbilical cord. Often the baby can be encouraged to turn in the last few weeks of pregnancy, by a doctor or midwife, but if not, labour will generally proceed as normal.

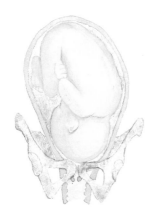

Anterior presentation

If your baby adopts this birth position, the head faces your back as it emerges, then turns immediately.

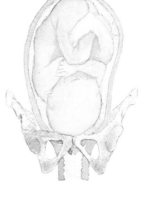

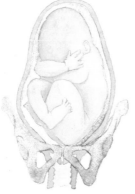

Breech position

If your baby lies bottom-down, you can still expect a normal, uncomplicated labour. But you will need experienced assistance to ensure that your baby's head is delivered safely. You may have backache, which some gentle massage can often ease.

Posterior presentation

If your baby faces forward in the early stages of labour, the head often turns into the usual backward-facing position in time for birth. You will feel slightly more strain on your lower back in early labour.

LABOUR

From the first contraction to after the birth

Every birth is unique and every woman's experience of it is personal to her. However, labour always follows the same pattern, which can be divided into three stages: stage one, when contractions cause the cervix, or neck of the womb, to soften and dilate, followed by transition, when the cervix becomes fully open; stage two, the birth itself; and stage three, the delivery of the placenta. The first stage may take anything up to 24 hours, but after this the baby may be born within an hour or two. A mother-to-be needs to be able to follow her instincts and feel free to move into any position she finds comfortable, breathing intuitively through each contraction. In the following pages we suggest some safe and helpful positions for each stage of labour, some for the woman to try alone, others that require the support of her partner.

STAGE ONE

The baby prepares to be born

During the first stage of labour, the womb contracts and the neck of the womb, the cervix, is drawn open to allow the baby to pass through. This can take from one to twenty-four hours, although six to twelve hours is more usual for a first child and even less for a second. When labour first begins, a woman will feel mild contractions, each lasting for about half a minute. These gradually become more regular and more intense, until they come every three to four minutes and last for one-and-a-half minutes. Each contraction pushes your baby down on to the cervix, until at the end of the first stage, it is dilated to a width of four or five fingers or 4 in (10cm). Continuing to breathe calmly and rhythmically, and remaining upright and active for as long as possible, will help to ease the contractions and allow gravity to encourage the baby's descent. Walking around between contractions can improve both circulation and stamina.

The effect of contractions

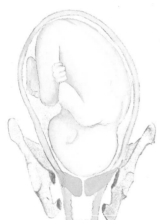

1 At the beginning of labour, the cervix at the base of the womb needs to stretch before the baby can pass through. As the womb contracts, it gradually pulls up the edges of the cervix, causing it to soften, stretch, and open.

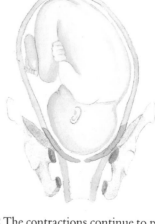

2 The contractions continue to push the baby down, against the thinning layer of the cervix.

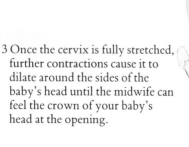

3 Once the cervix is fully stretched, further contractions cause it to dilate around the sides of the baby's head until the midwife can feel the crown of your baby's head at the opening.

Positions for stage one

A variety of positions will help to
ease the contractions, particularly
if the man supports his partner's
weight and massages her lower
back, while she blows gently on
the out-breath. Kneeling and
squatting usually relieve strain,
but the woman should allow her
own intuition to guide her.

Supported standing position

♀ *With your feet well apart and
your knees slightly bent, put your
arms around your partner's neck,
letting him support some of your
weight as he strokes your back.*
♂ *Stand with your feet well apart
and, with your partner's arms
around your neck, gently massage
her upper back.*

Supported squat

♀ *Squat on the floor with your
knees apart and clasp your hands
around your partner's neck,
breathing with your abdomen.*
♂ *Kneel in front of your partner,
draw her to you, and massage her
lower back.*

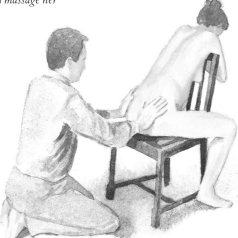

Sitting position

♀ *Take the weight off your feet by
sitting astride a chair, with your
arms resting on the back of the chair.*
♂ *Kneel down behind your partner
and gently massage her back,
concentrating on the area around the
base of the spine.*

TRANSITION
The cervix opens

Transition is the waiting phase between stage one, when the cervix is almost dilated and stage two, when the baby is ready to pass through the fully opened birth canal. The urge to push during transition is often strong but it is essential to wait until the cervix is fully dilated – the midwife will guide you if you are unsure. Many women find this a difficult time and become tired and irritable. Even though he may have to bear the brunt of her frustration, the man can help by remaining calm and reminding his partner that transition does not last and is only a step away from birth. Some women prefer to be left alone, others want close physical contact and support. But either way, what a woman needs most is for her partner to respond equably to her requests. At this stage, Light breathing (see p.37), with the emphasis on the out-breath, and experimenting with positions can help to redirect the powerful urge to push.

The cervix dilates

1 At transition, the end of stage one, the cervix is fully dilated, giving the baby's head access to the vaginal opening.

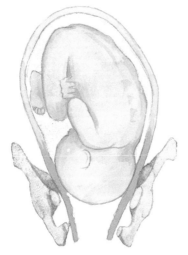

2 By the end of transition and the beginning of stage two, the baby's head has passed through the cervix into the vagina.

Positions for transition

The woman may prefer to be
left alone to get comfortable,
but the man can help by
distracting her attention from
the sensation of bearing down
and encouraging her to practise
Light breathing.

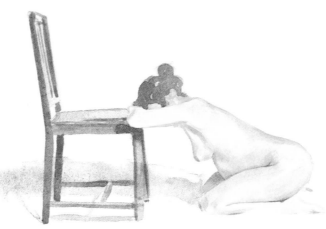

Kneeling position

♀ *Kneel forward with your knees
apart and your arms and forehead
resting on the edge of a chair. Keep
your back straight and stay as
upright as possible, to ease the
descent of the baby.*

Horizontal kneeling position

♀ *If the urge to bear down is very
strong, kneel down on the floor or
bed and lean right forward with
your forehead on a cushion and
your buttocks raised. But try not
to stay in this position for more
than a few minutes, since it may
delay birth.*

Lying position

♀ *Lie on your side on the bed,
with your top knee bent forward
and supported by a cushion.*

STAGE TWO

The baby is born

The birth itself, known as stage two, is the most rewarding and exhilarating part of labour. It can last from a few minutes to a couple of hours, but often takes between thirty and forty minutes. This is the time when the woman's intuition, the midwife's experience, and the man's support combine to ensure the safety of mother and baby. Powerful contractions now start at the top of the womb at two- to five-minute intervals, pushing the baby down until the urge to bear down engulfs the whole body. Breathing deeply and pushing on the out-breath is often suggested to utilize each contraction and help the woman to maximize her effort. The most natural position for giving birth is an upright one, since it leaves the pelvic joints free to open, stretches the pelvic floor muscles and allows gravity to assist the descent of the baby.

The baby's progress

1 At the beginning of the second stage, the baby is in position in the birth canal. After around 15-20 minutes, the baby's head appears at the opening of the vagina, stretching it as it begins to push its way through.

2 Each contraction pushes the head further out until it finally squeezes through. It rotates immediately, allowing the body to turn for birth.

3 After a few minutes' rest, a single contraction gives the baby a final push. The shoulders slide through one after the other, followed by the rest of the body.

Positions for stage two

The position in which a woman gives birth should be a matter of personal choice. Most women find a semi-upright position the most comfortable, especially when the man can take some of the strain. One of the following positions may prove helpful.

Supported kneeling position

♀ Kneel with your legs wide apart and your back against your partner's legs.
♂ Stand behind your partner. Slide your hands under her arms, clasp them around her chest and support her weight as she pushes.

Supported squat

♂ Kneel upright, with your back straight, pass your hands under your partner's arms and clasp them round her chest.
♀ Squat with your knees wide, and lean back against your partner.

Supported sitting position

♀ Sit on the edge of the bed with your knees spread wide, and lean back against your partner, allowing his arms to support some of your weight. The midwife can then receive the baby.
♂ Kneel down on the bed behind your partner, slip your arms under hers, and clasp your hands over her chest to support her.

4 ♀ If you feel overpowered by the contractions and feel the need to slow down the descent of the baby – and if the midwife confirms that the birth is straightforward – kneel with your knees apart, lean forward, and hold on to your partner's arms.
♂ Kneel down and sit back on your heels. Bend your arms and support your partner's outstretched arms.

5 ♀ If, as in 4, you wish to slow down the descent of your baby, but your partner is not with you, adopt an all-fours position, with your knees wide apart. The midwife will receive the baby from behind.

6 ♀ If your partner is not with you and you feel no need to slow down the descent of the baby, try sitting down with your back well-supported with cushions. Spread your knees and pull them toward you each time you push.

STAGE THREE

The placenta is delivered

♀ In an uncomplicated birth, your newborn baby should take its first breaths with the umbilical cord still intact. While you hold and suckle your baby, the third stage of labour may begin, as eye contact, skin contact and suckling help to stimulate further contractions that expel the placenta. To give yourself and especially your baby "breathing space" in the moments after birth, you should make a prior agreement with your hospital or midwife well before the birth, firstly, to wait until your baby is breathing and the umbilical cord no longer pulsates before cutting the cord, and secondly, not to stimulate the release of the placenta artificially with a hormone injection. To be fully informed and prepared for this stage, contact your community midwife, or a national childbirth organization.

The release of the placenta

Your baby helps to stimulate the release of the placenta by sucking at your breast. Sitting (right) or squatting (left) encourages the delivery of the placenta, and as it comes away, you may feel a warm, soothing sensation followed by shivering as your body readjusts. Try to keep yourself and your baby warm.

4

THE NEW BABY

Within the womb, the baby is surrounded by the mother. Warm and secure in her embrace, soothed by her sounds and movements, and constantly nourished, the unborn child has every need met from moment to moment. This safe existence is abruptly interrupted by the upheaval of birth, however, and in the vulnerable time that follows, the newborn baby needs to be reassured that the loving attention he or she was conditioned to receive in the womb will continue.

Touch is a baby's first language and the mother and father who kiss and cuddle their newborn baby help him or her to make the transition from the womb to the world with the minimum of anxiety. The baby's urgent need for close physical contact arouses the woman's instincts as a mother to feed and look after her child. But physical affection in this pre-verbal period can also influence your child's future emotional development. Children learn to love by being loved, especially when they are at their most vulnerable and insecure, and affectionate touch helps them to feel loved and valued for themselves, unconditionally, not for what they can do. Parents who relate to their children with physical warmth and love find it easier to maintain a peaceful, cohesive friendship with them in the future, and at the same time reinforce their children's natural ability to form loving relationships and to relate to the world as they grow up. Such emotional support is an essential source of security that lends babies the confidence they need to develop. A demonstrative relationship also has a positive influence on a child's physical development. The rhythms of respiration, digestion, and circulation, for example, which can be disrupted by stress and anxiety, all benefit from physical relaxation.

In some cultures, in parts of India and Malaya and amongst the Eskimos, for example, massage is included in the daily routine of childcare. Goodwill and affection are thus combined in a pleasurable activity that allows both parents and baby to get used to the feel of one another. Performed with love and care and with the emphasis on enjoyment, massaging your baby is highly therapeutic and promotes all the advantages of good health, while cultivating a relationship of mutual trust. In this chapter we outline the baby's physical development in the three months after birth, suggest comfortable positions for breastfeeding, and offer a gentle baby massage routine.

BREASTFEEDING

Comfortable positions for feeding your baby

♀ The most natural way of maintaining a close relationship with your baby is to breastfeed. Not only is the
physical contact emotionally gratifying for you both but
breast milk is the perfect food in the early days. It con-
tains all the protein, vitamins and antibodies a baby needs
for healthy development. Strong sucking stimulates
your breasts to produce milk on demand, but a relaxed,
stress-free atmosphere is also important as it encourages
this natural response. It is usually easier to establish a
satisfying pattern of breastfeeding if you put your baby
to the breast within a few minutes of birth. How long
you continue is a matter of personal choice. In America,
most children are weaned at six months, in Europe at
about a year, in Africa and Asia at around three years and
in Greenland and Mongolia at about four.

The let-down reflex

1 Glands within each breast enlarge
during pregnancy and release milk
into channel-like ducts, which
open out into small reservoirs
behind the nipple openings.

2 When sucking, your baby's
tongue and gums press on the
surround of the nipple. This
pressure draws milk from the
reservoirs into your baby's
mouth, and simultaneously
triggers the pituitary gland to
stimulate the release of more milk
into the ducts. The supply system
is designed to satisfy demand.

Normal breastfeeding

Sit cross-legged, with your back straight. Lay your baby sideways on your lap and hold him or her to your breast. Or if you prefer, sit on a chair, resting one foot on a stool to avoid back strain. You may need a pillow to raise your baby to breast height.

Breastfeeding twins

It may be easier to feed twins together than to double the number of feeds. Put two large cushions on your lap and lay both babies on top, facing you. Tuck one twin under each arm and cradle a head in each hand. If only one twin is crying, feed that one first, then wake and feed the other.

Breastfeeding after a caesarian

If your stomach is sore after stitches, lie down on your side, propped up on a pillow and lay your baby down beside you with his or her feet next to your pillow, well away from your stomach. This is also a good position for feeding at night.

Caution:
Always hold your baby's body close to you when you breastfeed, so that the head is not twisted.

EARLY DEVELOPMENT

From 0 to 3 months

Newborn babies can sleep almost round the clock. During waking moments, they suck, swallow and hiccup, and respond to touch, sounds and smells. Within the first month, they also begin to focus more clearly. Initially, the new baby displays a variety of reflexes, including walking motions with the legs and a grasping action with the hands, but these disappear as conscious movement develops. In the first three months, your baby will begin to unfold from a curled fœtal position and, through stretching its limbs, will open up the hip, shoulder, knee, and elbow joints. Simultaneously, head and neck control will increase as the back muscles become stronger and more co-ordinated, and as the spine begins to straighten. At the end of three months, most babies can support their upper bodies in a "cobra" position (*see opposite*) and, when supported in a standing position, can begin to bear some of their own weight.

Physical progress

In the first few months, young babies lie on their backs, their sides or their tummies. As the muscles in the neck and upper back grow stronger, the baby gradually learns to control the head. Until this time, however, always support the back of your baby's head when you lift and carry him or her.

Lying on the back

On their backs, babies will spontaneously stretch their bodies and extend their arms and legs. These movements gradually become more vigorous and controlled, and by 3 months, babies will kick with alternate legs and clasp their hands over their chests.

Lying on the side

A good intermediary position, lying on their sides will strengthen babies' neck and shoulder muscles. Your baby will need your help to roll from front to back until around the sixth month, however.

Lying on the tummy

Most babies feel secure when lying on their tummies. This position helps digestion by gently stretching and relaxing the abdominal muscles, and encourages babies to start lifting their heads.

The cobra position

By three months, babies will usually bear their weight on their hands, raising their shoulders up in the "cobra" position, with their legs well stretched out behind them. At the same time, they may begin to arch their backs and raise their feet.

BABY MASSAGE

A relaxing routine for mother and baby

♀ A regular baby massage in the weeks that follow birth will help to relax your baby and will give you the opportunity to get close to each other. Most parents find themselves instinctively stroking their babies and usually enjoy extending this natural response into a more complete massage routine. Massage helps to warm and relax the soft tissues of the body and can be practised by both the father and the mother. It is meant to be a pleasure for both you and your baby, but this can only be achieved with the full co-operation of the baby. Ensure that your hands are warm and relaxed before you start and only use natural oils, or calendula powder, to avoid irritating your baby's sensitive skin. The increased contact between you can be especially helpful if you are not breastfeeding, but avoid this sequence immediately after a heavy feed.

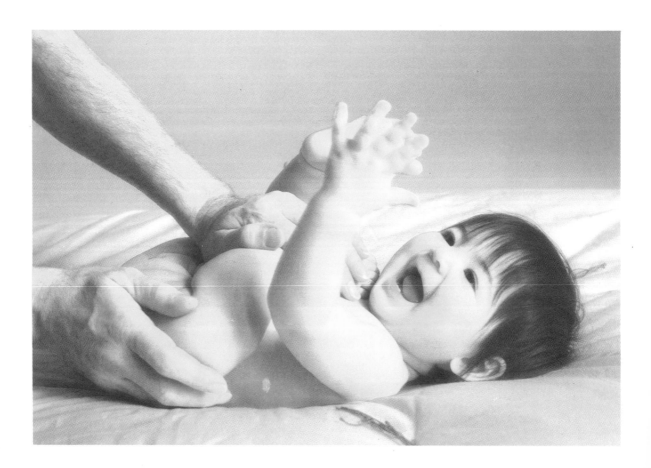

Back and spine

Gentle massage, combined with the appropriate postures, is soothing for babies and encourages them to co-ordinate their back muscles. Resting them on your chest or legs, or half seated against your inner thigh, will help them to lift their heads and strengthen neck and shoulder muscles.

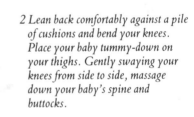

1 Sit comfortably, half reclining, against a pile of cushions. Rest your baby tummy-down on your chest and massage gently down the spine and buttocks, using both hands.

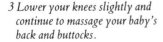

2 Lean back comfortably against a pile of cushions and bend your knees. Place your baby tummy-down on your thighs. Gently swaying your knees from side to side, massage down your baby's spine and buttocks.

3 Lower your knees slightly and continue to massage your baby's back and buttocks.

4 Straighten your knees and open your legs wide. Then lay your baby sideways over your thigh, supporting the head and lower back. This strengthens the back muscles, opens the chest and gently stretches the tummy.

Hips, tummy, arms and legs

Massaging the front of the body opens the chest, stretches the tummy muscles and helps breathing and digestion. The following exercises combine massage with postures that encourage your baby to stretch and relax the pelvic floor and extend the arms and legs. This improves flexibility throughout the lower body.

1 Sit comfortably against a cushion and raise your knees. Rest your baby on his or her back, on your thighs. Gently sway your legs and gradually open your baby's knees, pressing the soles of the feet against your abdomen.

2 Cup one hand and lay it lightly on your baby's tummy. Using the heel and fingers of your hand squeeze very softly on each side of the tummy. Then roll the tummy very gently from side to side, by pressing with the heel of your hand and pulling with your fingers.

3 Lift your baby and bring the soles of your feet together. Sit your baby on the cushion between your legs, with the head and back well supported by your body, and the soles of the feet together. This gently relaxes the inside thigh and tests the symmetry of the hips.

4 Lift your baby on to your lap and raise your left leg, so that your baby can recline sideways against it. Without rushing, encourage your baby to lift one arm, but don't try to straighten it. Gently squeeze down the arm and stroke down the side of the chest. Repeat on both sides.

5 Straighten your legs and turn your baby so that he or she can lean back against your abdomen. Again, without rushing, encourage your baby to stretch one leg, but don't try to straighten it. Repeat the exercise on both sides.

5

GETTING FIT

Sensation and movement are two of life's greatest gifts and once mobile, your child will explore them to the full. Lifting, swinging, chasing, catching and carrying your infant place increasing demands on your body's health and resources, so if you are to fulfil your child's physical needs with the minimum of stress and strain and with maximum pleasure, you will need to be in relatively good shape. This chapter includes guidelines for maintaining good posture when you have small children, postnatal exercises to help the woman tone up her muscles, and a forty-minute fitness programme for both parents.

After adolescence, when the body is fully formed, there is no physical development without effort and the muscles and joints need consistent exercise to maintain ease and mobility. Stiffness and inflexibility are the first signs of physical deterioration, and are the body's long-term response to muscular tension accumulated over the years as a result of emotional and physical stress. Tension can begin in childhood, and if left untended, slowly reduces the body's range of movement, creates postural imbalance and impairs the quality of adult life.

Ancient physicians, such as the Greek, Hippocrates, maintained that the body is in good health when there is a good bodily feeling, when it feels no "dis-ease". This condition is reflected outwardly in a balanced, well-shaped body, capable of a wide range of strong, graceful movements, and inwardly by good humour and a sense of optimism. As a result, these early physicians encouraged people to exercise, in the knowledge that fit people are healthy people and healthy people are happy. Dynamic sports improve strength and stamina, but need to be combined with flexibility exercises if they are not to reinforce a wrong pattern of movement.

Stretching is our body's natural response to a cramped position, to relieve tension in our muscles and joints. Every young baby uncurls after birth, and we all instinctively stretch our limbs after waking from a good night's sleep. By urging the muscles to release their grip on the joints, stretching restores flexibility and at the same time encourages a free, revitalizing flow of blood to the muscles as they relax. Flexibility exercises not only realign your body's joints, improve shape and posture and benefit circulation and respiration, they also ensure that you relax properly, both when you are active and when you rest.

GOOD POSTURE

Preventing physical stress

A balanced posture conserves energy, reduces muscular effort and eliminates strain. As mechanical law explains: the closer to the centre of gravity weight is maintained, the less effort is required for it to remain upright. With a well-centred structure, the muscles, relieved of the job of supporting an imbalanced weight, are free to move the body in a more relaxed way. This in turn benefits the body's vital organs, such as the heart and lungs and the digestive and nervous systems. The finest examples of good posture are seen in children. An infant, for instance, will sit comfortably on the backs of the thighs, rather than on the buttocks and lower back. This eliminates lower back strain and allows the spine to remain straight and to counterbalance the weight it supports. We can safeguard our backs and joints by consciously lifting, sitting, standing, and moving with our weight well centred, and bending from the knees and hips.

Good standing posture

Many children naturally adopt a good posture, setting an example for many adults. With the back straight, the hips tilted forward, the knees slightly flexed and the feet apart, the weight passes evenly through the weight-bearing joints to the heels and arches of the feet. This natural posture holds the body upright through balance, instead of muscular effort.

Breastfeeding with a straight back

Sit with your legs comfortably crossed, and feel your weight well centred beneath you. Then, straighten your back and shoulders, as if the top of your head is being drawn up, and feed your baby. You may need a pillow to support the baby.

Lifting your child

1 Bend your knees and squat down
with your feet well apart and your
back straight. Hold your child
around the ribs and lift with your
elbows flexed and your child's head
level with your own. Always avoid
bending with straight legs.

2 Straighten your legs until you are
upright and keep your shoulders
well squared, as you lift your child.

3 As you come fully upright, keep
your back straight and hold your
child close to your chest, with the
head well supported.

TONE-UP

Solo postnatal exercises

♀ Giving birth is demanding and strenuous – both emotionally and physically. After all the anticipation, and the joy and excitement that accompany birth, it is not unusual for a woman to suffer from fatigue and postnatal blues in the days or weeks that follow. Adequate rest, a nutritious diet and your partner's active support will all speed your recovery. Warm, slightly salt baths taken frequently are not only soothing, but help to heal any tears, cuts or grazes. After a few days, you will begin to resume light activities and when all bleeding and discomfort have ceased, you will be ready to get back into shape. The following flexibility exercises will help to restore your muscle tone, especially in the abdominal and pelvic floor muscles, which need to regain their tone after rigorously stretching during birth. They combine well with pelvic floor exercises (see p. 35).

Solo exercises

This routine is best practised on a soft surface, preferably on your bed. Hold each posture for a minute or two, while practising Abdominal breathing (see p.29) and massaging the area you are exercising. You can also include your baby in this exercise routine.

1 Kneel down and open your knees as wide as you can. Gradually lean forward on to your elbows and relax. As you rock slowly to and fro, gently contract and relax your pelvic floor (see p.35).

2 Sit with your knees open and the soles of your feet together. Support your baby between your legs and, as you gently rock from side to side, contract and relax your pelvic floor.

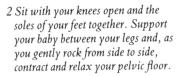

Caution:
If you feel any back pain, stop and sit more upright.

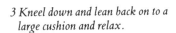

3 Kneel down and lean back on to a large cushion and relax.

4 Stand facing the bed with your legs wide. Lift your buttocks as you lean gently forward, resting your hands or elbows on the bed. Come upright again, then bring your feet closer together, and once again lift your buttocks as you lean forward again on to the bed.

5 Kneel on the bed and slide your
arms forward. Slowly bring your
head and chest to the bed, lifting
your buttocks as you do so. Hold for
a moment, then relax.

6 Lie on your front, with your chin
resting on your hands. Relax your
abdomen and contract and relax your
pelvic floor several times.

7 Put your hands under your
shoulders and lift up, supporting
your weight on your hands. As you
breathe out, tighten your buttocks,
tilt your head back and push your
chest forward. Then gently lower
yourself.

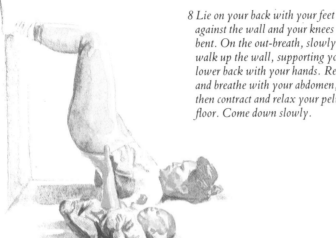

8 Lie on your back with your feet against the wall and your knees bent. On the out-breath, slowly walk up the wall, supporting your lower back with your hands. Relax, and breathe with your abdomen, then contract and relax your pelvic floor. Come down slowly.

9 Lie on your back with your head on a pillow. Bring your knees together and rest your baby, tummy-down on your lower legs. Holding your baby's hands slowly raise your legs, pulling them in toward your abdomen to stretch your lower back. Then slowly lower your legs.

Caution:
If you feel back pain in any of these positions, come slowly down and rest.

10 Now lay your baby on your right side, within the crook of your arm. Twisting from the hips, lower your legs over to the left and place your left hand on your right knee and relax. Repeat on the other side. Then slowly come back to the centre and rest.

S T R E T C H I N G

A forty-minute fitness programme

The mobility of your muscles and joints is the true test of their health and fitness. These stretching exercises not only reveal hidden stiffness and inflexibility but also gradually encourage the muscles to relax with ease. Reducing stiffness also has a far-reaching effect on general health. Maintaining the flexibility of your back, for example, enhances the health of the vital organs; relieving tension in the neck and shoulders helps to remove the underlying cause of many headaches; and flexible hips, knees and ankles can prevent structural compensations from throwing the entire body out of line. The following programme offers an easy and effective sequence for both parents to practise together or alone. Wear loose, comfortable clothes, and don't eat immediately before exercise. Begin by spending two minutes in each position, slowly building up to five minutes.

Hips, knees and ankles

The muscles and joints of the legs and feet which carry most of the body's weight are inevitably prone to stiffness. The flexibility of the hips also influences the health of the spinal column.

1 Sit on the edge of a cushion, or with your lower back firmly against the wall. Open your knees and bring the soles of your feet together. Relax in this position, breathing with your abdomen.

2 With your feet still together, breathe in, and on the out-breath gently push one knee toward the floor. Massage your inside thigh and knee; relax in this position, breathing with your abdomen. Repeat with the other knee.

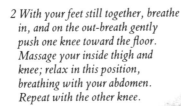

3 With your feet still together, hold your ankles and breathe in. On the out-breath, gently push your knees down with your elbows. Relax, breathing with your abdomen.

4 Kneel down with your knees together and breathe in. On the out-breath, lean backward, resting your weight on your hands.

5 Tighten your buttocks to protect your lower back. Breathe in, and on the out-breath, slowly push your pelvis forward and up. Relax in this position, breathing with your abdomen, then slowly lower your pelvis and sit down.

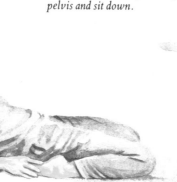

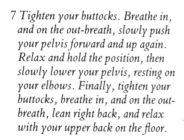

6 Tighten your buttocks. Breathe in, and on the out-breath, tilt your pelvis forward and lean back on to your elbows. Relax in this position, breathing with your abdomen.

Caution:
If you experience back pain in any of these positions, open your knees. Always come back up slowly from these positions.

7 Tighten your buttocks. Breathe in, and on the out-breath, slowly push your pelvis forward and up again. Relax and hold the position, then slowly lower your pelvis, resting on your elbows. Finally, tighten your buttocks, breathe in, and on the out-breath, lean right back, and relax with your upper back on the floor.

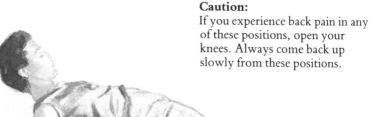

8 *Squat with your feet about 2 ft (60cm) apart, heels raised. Put your hands on the floor with your elbows inside your knees. On an out-breath, gently push your knees open with your elbows. Relax, and holding this position, breathe with your abdomen.*

9 *Still squatting, breathe in, and on the out-breath, gently push your knees open with your elbows and bring your heels to the floor. Relax, intermittently contracting and relaxing the muscles of your anus and pelvic floor.*

10 *On an out-breath, slowly begin to straighten your legs to come up into a forward bend. Loosely fold your arms and keep your neck and shoulders relaxed. Relax while you hold this position, breathing with your abdomen.*

11 *Breathe in, and on the out-breath, slowly straighten one leg. Massage any area that feels stiff. Relax while you hold this position, breathing with your abdomen. Then repeat with the other leg.*

12 *Place your hands flat on the floor and relax your neck and shoulders. As you breathe out, straighten both legs, pushing your weight back as far as you can and lifting your buttocks. Hold this position, then release and massage your legs.*

13 *Slowly separate your feet until they are about 4 ft (1·2m) apart and turn your toes inward. Rest your hands on your lower back and hold the position. Massage any muscles that feel stiff.*

14 *Reach your hands down to the floor. On an out-breath, straighten both legs, keeping your feet firmly on the floor. Relax in this position and, breathing with your abdomen, rock backward and forward.*

15 *Open your legs wider, keeping your feet turned inward. On an out-breath, lower your elbows to the floor and lift your buttocks, relaxing your neck and shoulders. To release, bend your knees and stand up.*

Back, belly, chest and shoulders

The back is the central support for all the body's organs, the limbs and the head; the spine is held erect by the strength of its supporting muscles. Stretching the front of the body helps to counteract the effect of the abdominal muscles pulling the chest and shoulders forward.

1 Sit upright and curl your right foot around your left buttock. Take your left foot over your right knee to the floor. On an out-breath, pull your left knee toward you with your right arm. Turn your head and shoulders to the left, and put your left hand on the floor behind you. Keep your back straight and relax.

2 On an out-breath, rotate further and put your right hand on the floor in front of your right shin. Keeping your back straight, relax. Repeat 1 and 2 on the other side.

Caution:

If you feel back pain at any point, stop the exercise and adopt a comfortable, supported position and relax. Always come slowly out of these positions.

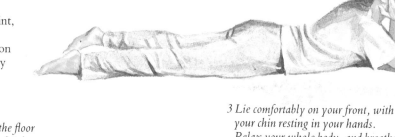

3 Lie comfortably on your front, with your chin resting in your hands. Relax your whole body, and breathe with your abdomen.

4 Put your hands flat on the floor under your shoulders and tighten your buttocks. On an out-breath, gently raise your chest from the floor. Lean your head back, hold, breathing with your abdomen, then slowly come down to the floor.

5 Stand an arm's length from the wall, raise your arms and rest your hands against the wall. Tighten your buttocks, and, on an out-breath, push your chest forward. Arching your back, rest your head against the wall.

6 On an out-breath, push firmly from the base of your hands. Lift your head and arch your upper back, bringing your breastbone against the wall.

Caution:
If you feel any pain in your back or neck during any of these exercises, stop and rest.

7 Turn around with your back to the wall, tighten your buttocks and breathe in. On an out-breath, arch your back, lift your arms, and put your palms against the wall, keeping your knees flexed.

8 On an out-breath, walk away from the wall, keeping your buttocks, back and shoulder muscles tight. Straighten your arms and keep the knees flexed. Hold the position for a few steady breaths then slowly walk back toward the wall, bringing your arms down to your side .

Head, neck and shoulders

Stiffness in the neck, one of the most common sites of tension, often spreads across the top of the shoulders. If the upper back weakens and allows the shoulders to become rounded, the neck then cramps in order to keep the head balanced.

Caution:
If you feel any pain in your neck or back during any of these exercises, stop and rest.

1 Lie on your back, raise your legs and bring your knees to your forehead as you support your back with your hands. Relax, breathing with your abdomen.

2 With your buttocks tight, straighten your legs until they are in line with your head in a shoulder-stand. Relax, breathing with your abdomen.

3 Lower your left leg forward over your head and your right leg back until you are doing the splits. Relax, breathing with your abdomen.

4 Lower your left leg to the floor and bring your right leg up in line with your head. Relax, breathing with your abdomen. Repeat exercises 3 and 4 with the other leg, then come back into a shoulder-stand.

5 With your legs straight, take your feet over your head to the floor. Extend your arms behind your back and clasp your hands. Relax, breathing with your abdomen. Take a deep breath and unroll very slowly on the out-breath. Relax.

6 Sit back on your heels with your back straight and your chin tucked in. Lower your left ear to your left shoulder. Then wrap your left arm over your head and rest your hand on your ear. Relax, breathing with your abdomen, using the weight of your arm to increase the stretch.

7 With your arm still cradling your head, gently massage your neck with your other hand. Repeat 6 and 7 on the other side.

8 Lean back, and rest your weight on your hands. Push your chest forward and slowly push out your chin as you tilt your head backward, to stretch your throat from your jaw to your collarbone. Hold this position, then slowly sit up.

6
BECOMING A TODDLER

Between three and fifteen months, babies become mobile, learning to sit, then to crawl, to stand and eventually to walk unaided. Since physical development precedes speech, every baby of this age needs to be assured of love and goodwill through physical contact and companionship. Play-oriented exercises, involving you and your child, are highly therapeutic when children are so emotionally and physically responsive. This shared movement not only encourages you to handle your child with confidence and so inspires trust, but also allows the child to maximize his or her potential range of mobility.

Time spent practising playful exercises is time well spent in getting to know your baby, and discovering how he or she likes to be touched, held and moved. This also gives you the opportunity to learn about your baby's muscles, bones and joints and their various movements, and so helps them to develop relaxed strength and flexibility.

Exercises that stretch and strengthen the body evenly at this stage promote balance and good posture. This in turn helps to ensure that all the major muscles and joints function more fully and with more ease, both now and later. Posture also influences the other major systems of the body, including the heart, lungs, digestive and nervous systems. By encouraging your baby to develop a well-balanced physique at this stage, through simple shared exercises, you are helping to establish optimum conditions for a healthy future.

This chapter offers an outline of your baby's physical development, from three to fifteen months, as well as a sequence of playful exercises – Soft Gymnastics – especially intended for fathers and babies. These can be practised whenever you and your child feel receptive to them, and provide a starting point from which to develop your own variations, based on the guidance we give here, and your baby's pleasurable responses. Babies should be allowed to follow each stage of their natural physical development at their own pace. The exercises are progressive and it is important to ensure that your baby is emotionally and physically prepared before continuing to each new stage, so that the nervous system is ready to cope with new movements. Given time, and the right approach, your baby will enjoy and anticipate this kind of activity. Eventually, he or she will perform similar exercises spontaneously and will begin to explore new movements.

From 3 to 15 months

Development is a continuous and natural process and every baby follows the same pattern of physical accomplishment, sitting up, crawling, standing, walking and so on. All babies, however, acquire these physical skills in their own time, and the precise age at which they do so is no reflection on their intelligence. Between three and seven months, babies develop the movements of the head and neck, hands, arms and shoulders and enough strength and co-ordination in the back to sit upright. Between seven months and a year, they have usually developed enough strength and co-ordination in the lower body to crawl in some fashion. Between a year and fifteen months or later, babies gain the strength and balance to stand and to walk, often unaided.

Becoming mobile

As your baby learns to sit, stand and walk unaided, you can help by encouraging new movements. Putting your infant into new positions, for example, will give him or her the opportunity to explore and discover new ways of moving independently.

Sitting up

Between three and seven months the back muscles grow strong enough to allow the baby to sit upright. He or she will soon be able to lean forward, holding the toes in a flexible sitting position.

Crawling

Once sitting, after around seven months, many babies pull themselves over on to all fours and start to crawl, enjoying their first taste of independent movement. Some children, however, prefer to miss out much of the crawling stage.

Standing while holding on

Between seven months and a year, the baby learns to stand on two feet. You can encourage your baby to perfect this posture and to practise balancing by arranging furniture of the correct height around the house for him or her to hold on to.

Taking the first steps

Once standing unaided, your baby will soon gain the confidence to take the first few steps. With practice and encouragement, he or she will gradually gain the confidence and co-ordination to walk steadily and without support.

Climbing stairs

At around 12 to 15 months, babies love to climb stairs. If you have stairs at home, it is a good idea to encourage your baby to get used to going up and down unaided, while you are near, so that he or she learns to negotiate stairs safely and without fear.

Performing forward bends

Once your child is walking, he or she will be ready to follow up assisted exercises (see next page) with solo gymnastics (see pp. 106-115). From around 12 or 15 months, your child may be ready to start performing forward bends, first with your help, then unaided.

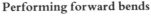

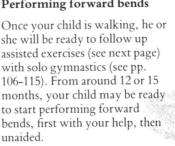

SOFT GYMNASTICS

Exercises for father and baby

♂ The following exercises help to cultivate a sense of confidence and trust between father and child, while sowing the seeds of health and fitness. They are easy to perform and, when practised with plenty of hugs, kisses and soft massage, become a series of affectionate games. These exercises encourage suppleness, flexibility and co-ordination throughout the body. This means that by the time your child is strong enough to stand and walk independently, with your help, he or she will have the kind of self-confidence that comes with a relaxed, flexible body. You can start each sequence when your child is about three months, but take your time, proceeding gradually and allowing the baby's pleasurable responses to guide you. Never practise exercises after a heavy feed or against your baby's wishes, especially when introducing new movements.

Arms and shoulders

One of the most instinctive movements we make every day is to stretch our arms to relieve tension in the arms, shoulders and upper chest. From about three months, babies lying on their tummies strengthen their upper bodies by pushing themselves upward. These exercises cultivate suppleness and flexibility in the arms and shoulders while they become stronger.

3 Months

Kneel down, with your baby's back against your abdomen. Hold the upper arms and gently lift them up and outward, then lightly shake them, using your fingers.

3 Months

As you feel the arms and shoulders relax, hug them against your chest. Once these two exercises become easy, combine them with massage, gently squeezing the arms and shoulders.

5 Months

Hold the forearms and, keeping the elbows in front of the body, slowly raise them in line with the shoulders, by leaning back and gently pulling then releasing the arms both together.

Still holding the forearms, lean back, and rock your baby, pulling and releasing very gently. Don't force it; all babies straighten their arms in their own time.

5 Months

6 Months

When the first four exercises become easy, hold your baby's forearms and kneel up, keeping your body in contact with the baby's back. Lift your baby momentarily and repeat two or three times.

Kneel comfortably and turn your baby around to face you. Holding the forearms, not the wrists, gently swing your baby backward and forward. Only keep your baby suspended momentarily.

9 Months

Hips, legs and feet

The baby's first step toward independence is to sit unaided, and this is made all the easier with flexible hips and knees. Once sitting, babies begin to strengthen their legs in earnest, for crawling, standing and walking. These exercises ensure that while the legs are strengthening, there is no stiffness in the movement of ankles, knees and hips.

Caution:
Don't force your baby's legs to straighten; this will happen when your baby is ready.

Kneel comfortably with your baby's legs astride your waist. Embrace your baby and massage the upper and lower back.

3 Months

Gently lay your baby back on to a soft surface, kiss and blow on both feet as you open the knees, and bring the soles of the feet together in line with the legs and hips, at right angles to the body. Gently rock your baby as you push the legs alternately to the left and the right.

3 Months

4 Months

As you feel the legs relax, slowly and gently guide both feet toward your baby's face. Gently rock the legs, and allow the lower back to leave the floor. Don't try to straighten your baby's knees.

6 Months

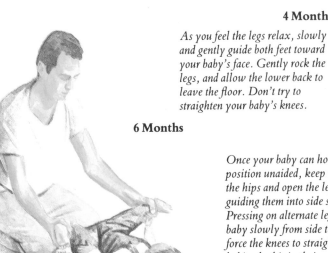

Once your baby can hold this position unaided, keep the feet above the hips and open the legs, gently guiding them into side splits. Pressing on alternate legs, rock your baby slowly from side to side. Don't force the knees to straighten; all babies do this in their own time.

Assume a comfortable position and sit your baby on the floor against you, with the knees wide open and the feet together, tucked well into the body.

3 Months

4 Months

Supporting the chest, encourage your baby to lean forward on to both hands. Once your baby can do this, he or she will only need practice to sit unaided.

Sitting the baby up straight, keep one knee bent and straighten the other leg sideways. Now reverse the position, straightening the other leg. Don't force it, and allow your baby to straighten the knees when he or she is ready.

6 Months

6 Months

Now encourage your baby to open both legs together, but don't force them.

4 Months

To encourage a perfect sitting posture, sit your baby on your lap, with the feet together and the knees apart. Keep your hands underneath your baby's arms and hold the legs.

4 Months

Supporting your baby's chest with your hands and forearms, and with the back resting against your abdomen, gently lift and bounce the baby two or three times.

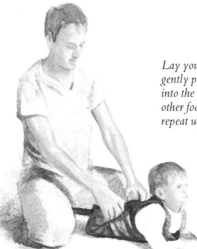

Lay your baby tummy-down and gently press the instep of one foot into the buttocks. Repeat with the other foot and, when comfortable, repeat with both feet together.

3 Months

6 Months

Encourage your baby to sit back between the feet, giving support under the arms. Then hold your baby's hands.

Caution:
Never force any movements against your baby's will.

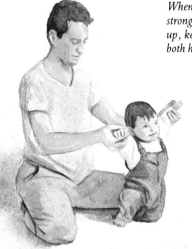

When your baby's head and back are strong, encourage him or her to stand up, keeping a supportive hold on both hands.

7 Months

8 Months

As your baby gets the feel of standing on two feet, maintain support under the arms.

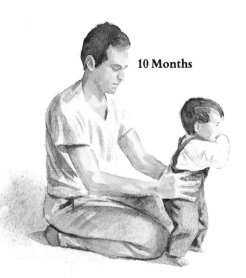

10 Months

Slowly lower your hands and support the hips, pushing gently downward to "anchor" the feet.

12 Months

If your baby is secure, support the thighs, moving downward. Slowly withdraw your hands and allow him or her to stand upright, unaided, for a few moments.

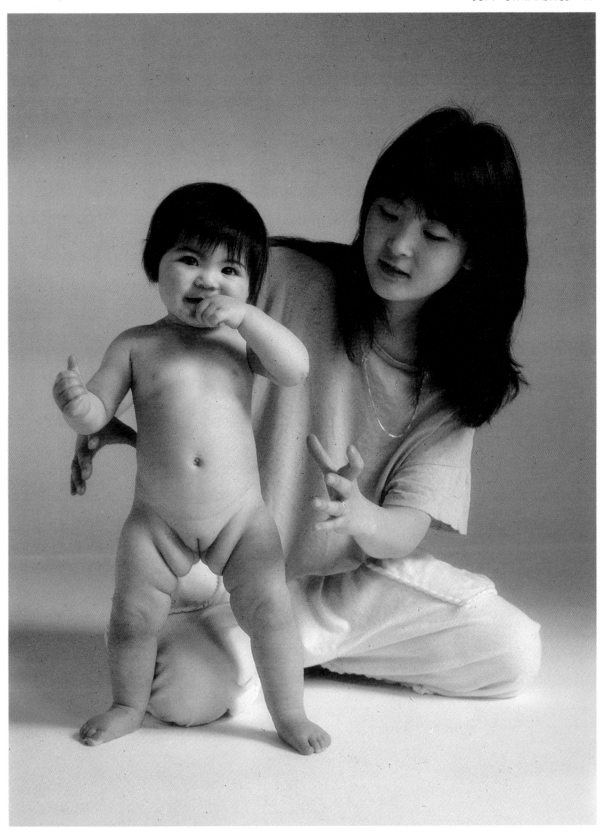

Back, chest and tummy

Having learned to hold and turn
the head and neck, the baby
develops strength and co-
ordination of the back and spine.
These exercises help to open the
chest and relax the abdominal
muscles, which in turn encourages good breathing and
digestive rhythms. They can also
be enhanced by lightly tapping the
chest and by soft massage of the
tummy.

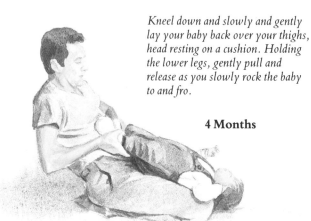

*Kneel down and slowly and gently
lay your baby back over your thighs,
head resting on a cushion. Holding
the lower legs, gently pull and
release as you slowly rock the baby
to and fro.*

4 Months

*Separate the legs and put them
around your waist or lift them and
let them open against your chest.
Lean forward and gently pat the
chest with both hands. Encourage
your baby to say "ahmm" and
"ehmm" so that the voice resonates.*

4 Months

4 Months

9 Months

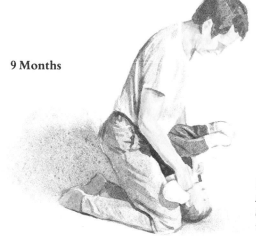

*Gently massage your baby's tummy
in a clockwise motion around the
navel, moving from left to right.*

*Put both hands on your baby's
shoulders and slowly lift up, tilting
the baby, controlling the movement
with your hands and arms.*

9 Months

Keeping a firm hold, slowly let your baby perform a backward roll, allowing the legs to pass through your arms toward the floor.

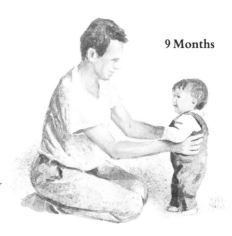

9 Months

As your baby balances back on two feet, support the body at the waist and congratulate and encourage your infant before continuing.

6 Months

With your baby lying back over your thighs, hold the lower legs firmly and raise up on to your knees, keeping the baby's body constantly in contact with yours as it tilts downward.

6 Months

Gently bring your child into a straight line and lift momentarily, then slowly sit back with your child lying back over your legs.

7
EARLY CHILDHOOD

Between fifteen months and three years old, young children develop rapidly, both physically and mentally, but they still at times need the same protective care, unconditional affection and encouragement as the babe-in-arms. These needs are recognized by traditional societies, such as the Ibos and the Onitshas of West Africa and the Aborigines of Australia who give great consideration to children under four. Adults in these cultures refuse to engage in battles of will and never resort to physical discipline, tending instead to admire children who exert themselves and stand their ground even against an adult. When a child strikes out against an adult in anger and frustration, it is shrugged off with good humour, for they understand that behind the will to succeed lies the spirit and to break the child's will can injure the spirit. The adults actively encourage children to climb, run and jump, and praise them for their efforts. As a result, their children grow up to be physically skilful and to feel entirely at home in their surroundings.

Young children are full of life, expressing their vitality with their entire bodies. Given the chance, they explore their physical abilities with great courage and a sense of adventure. Day to day, however, children are rarely encouraged to allow their bodies to test the full range of movements for which they were designed. For this reason, most children reach adolescence without having developed their natural physical potential, and even infants of five years or less often play within a restricted pattern of movement.

During these first few years, when children are at their most supple, exercises that complement balanced physical development are most effective. From around fifteen months, one of the most precious gifts a parent can give is to engage their toddler in physical games that are as pleasurable as they are beneficial. Without love and joy, exercise becomes a mechanical routine, but all children respond willingly and well if it is fun. As mobility and speech develop, so does the imagination, and infants love stories that conjure up an illusory realm full of imaginary characters, especially if they can join in. This chapter outlines the physical progress that occurs between fifteen months and three years, and presents Jungle Games, a story that introduces children to exercise through imaginative play and Jungle Gymnastics, a follow-up sequence for a child to perform with the help of an adult.

PHYSICAL DEVELOPMENT

From 15 months to 3 years

During this time, children perfect many physical skills, develop a large, intelligible vocabulary, ask countless questions and listen eagerly to stories. From the age of two, they run firmly on both feet, love to climb – given the chance – and join in nursery rhymes and simple stories. From around two and a half, they can jump, kick a ball, stand on tiptoes, scoot and steer mobile toys and negotiate stairs. Constantly asking questions, beginning with what, why and where, children can now repeat simple nursery rhymes and stories. From around three, they can climb skilfully, ride tricycles, balance on one leg and may jump from a chair on to a soft surface. At the same time they still ask a lot of questions and demand endless repeats of favourite stories.

Exploring new movement

Between fifteen months and three years, children become increasingly agile and enjoy the novelty of moving independently. Encourage your child's natural exuberance and try to create safe conditions so that he or she can play and explore new movements without anxiety.

Standing unaided

By fifteen months, children can generally balance well enough to stand steadily on two feet without support of any kind. Some children, however, stand well before their first birthday, others at nearer two.

Walking confidently

Once standing, a child will soon learn to walk without toppling, usually before the age of two. Allow your child to walk barefoot whenever possible and ensure that his or her first shoes fit well.

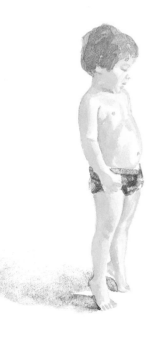

Standing on tiptoes

From around two and a half, the feet and postural muscles are usually sufficiently co-ordinated to allow the child to stand on tiptoes without overbalancing. The next step is to walk on tiptoes.

Standing on one leg

At around three years, your child will be able to balance on one leg for a few moments, and will soon be able to hold this position even when grasping a toy in one hand.

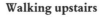

Jumping

From around three years, children delight in leaping off a low chair or bed on to a soft surface. Remember to keep unstable chairs out of reach.

Walking upstairs

Between two and three, most children learn to walk up and down stairs, putting two legs on each step at first. Encourage your child to practise going up and down stairs and keep watching until he or she is completely confident.

JUNGLE GAMES

A playful exercise routine

Yoga, one of the most effective forms of exercise, involves positions that imitate the natural poise and agility observed in animals. The following story is designed to encourage your child to copy the movements and postures of a selection of creatures. When practised as a sequence, the exercises will improve the relaxed strength and flexibility of all the major muscles and joints. The easiest approach is to read the story and familiarize your child with all the characters before you suggest he or she imitates one or two of the postures. You can then gradually build up until your child can perform the full range and enjoys miming each animal as you read through the entire story. Eventually, your child will adopt some of these postures spontaneously. You may prefer to use your child's own name, or to call the main character "Minnie Monkey" if you have a little girl.

Jungle story

Mickey Monkey wakes up in his bed in the treetops and looks out over the jungle. The sun is coming up and the birds are starting to sing. Mickey can see Stella Stork slowly lifting her head from under her wing and he knows it's time to get up. Mickey yawns and stretches then jumps out of his tree and lands next to his friend, Florence Frog.

"I was watching you jumping," says Mickey, "How do you jump so high?" "Well," says Florence, "First I crouch down like this". *Mickey crouches and leans forward.*

"Then I sit up and open my knees and straighten my back." *Mickey sits up, opens his knees and straightens his back.*

SPLOSH!

"And then I jump," says Florence. With that, Florence takes a great leap forward and disappears into the pond...

Mickey leaps so far that he lands at the other side of the pond next to Olga Ostrich.

"Hello Mickey. Come and listen to Humphrey Hedgehog snoring," says Olga. "Bend your knees and lean right forward." *Mickey bends his knees and leans right forward.* "Now put your head and hands on the floor and straighten your legs," says Olga. *Mickey puts his head and hands on the floor and straightens his legs.*

Mickey can hear Humphrey snoring. He looks through his legs and everything's turned upside down. *He straightens himself up.* "Come on Olga," says Mickey. "Let's go and wake up Humphrey, he's always the last to get up." "What's all this noise?" asks a sleepy voice.

Humphrey has woken up. "I must have overslept," he says. He climbs out of his hole among the stones and leaves and rolls all the way over to Mickey. "Hello," says Mickey, "Will you teach me how to do that?"

"Yes," says Humphrey. "First of all, squat down like Florence Frog." *Mickey squats down.* "Now put your hands on the floor, tuck your head in and roll over like this," says Humphrey as he rolls over.

Mickey put his hands on the floor, tucks in his head and rolls over...

and over...

and over...

He rolls so far that he bumps right into Bruno Bear...

BUMP

Bruno is sitting with his legs wide open and his honey pot beside him. "Hello Mickey," says Bruno. "Would you like some honey?" "Yes please," says Mickey. "Here, sit like this," says Bruno. *Mickey sits down and opens his legs as wide as he can.* "Good," says Bruno.

"Now lean forward and put your head right down on the ground." *Mickey leans forward and puts his head on the ground.* He lifts up his head and sees that Bruno has his head right inside the pot and is eating all the honey. "Save some for me!" says Mickey.

S L U R P

S L U R P

All of a sudden, Mickey hears a fluttering sound and looks up. It's Belinda Butterfly. "Hello Mickey," she says. "See if you can catch me!" Mickey gets up and runs after her, shouting, "Bye-bye, Bruno" as he goes...

At last Belinda comes to rest on a big leaf. "How do you fly like that?" asks Mickey. "Is it easy?" "Well," says Belinda. "It is for me." *Mickey thinks for a moment. Then he sits on the ground and opens his knees and holds his feet, pulling them together.*

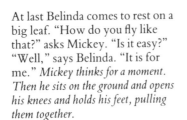

"Now flap your legs up and down like wings," says Belinda. *Mickey flaps his legs up and down and tries to fly after Belinda, but he still hasn't moved.*

G R U N T

Mickey is beginning to feel a bit tired by now, so he lays his head on his feet and closes his eyes. He nearly falls asleep, but a funny sound makes him jump.

When Mickey looks around, who should he see but his uncle, Godfrey Gorilla, sitting on a big rock by the river. "Hello Uncle Godfrey," says Mickey. "Hello Mickey. Come up and look at these lovely clouds," says Godfrey. Mickey climbs up on to the rock. "Kneel down and sit between your feet," says Godfrey. "I find it's by far the most comfortable way to sit." *Mickey kneels down and sits between his feet.*

Then he leans back and rests on his hands, looking at the clouds with his Uncle Godfrey. After a little while there's a loud snore. Godfrey Gorilla has fallen asleep.

Suddenly Mickey hears a loud sniffing sound…

SNIFF SNIFF

A head appears out of the grass.
It's Seymour Snake. He is lying
on the grass with his back arched
and his nose right up in the air.
"Hello Mickey," says Seymour.
"Can you smell food?"

*Mickey lies on his tummy next to
Seymour, puts his hands on the floor
and lifts his head, chest and shoulders
high in the air. He takes a few deep
sniffs of jungle air.*

S
N
I
F
F

"You'd make a good snake,
Mickey," says Seymour.
"Thanks, Seymour. Look, can
you do this?" says Mickey. *He lifts
his feet and tries to scratch the back of
his head with his toes.* Seymour tries
to lift his tail, but finds himself
just rolling round in the grass.

Mickey lies down and rests for a
moment. Then, feeling thirsty, he
gets up and walks down to the
river and squats at the water's
edge to drink.

"Having a nice day?" asks a quiet voice. It's Stella Stork, fishing for her dinner. "Yes, thank you. I've been leaping and rolling and flying like the other animals," says Mickey.

"See if you can stand like me," says Stella. "Oh, that's easy," says Mickey. *He lifts up one foot and tries to stand on one leg like Stella but finds it very difficult.* "You see," says Stella. "Sometimes the things that look easy are hardest of all!" "Yes," says Mickey. "What a clever stork you are".

Together they watch the sun disappear behind the trees. As the jungle grows quiet and still, Stella tucks her head under her wing and falls fast asleep. Mickey hears his mother calling from high up in the trees and runs off home to tell her about his adventures.

JUNGLE GYMNASTICS

Exercises for father and child

These gymnastic exercises follow on naturally from the simple postures included in Jungle Games and encourage your child to explore a wider range of movement. They are designed as a routine for you to practise with your child, whenever you are both in the mood for shared games. You may enjoy inventing variations on the animal theme, using the character of Mickey or Minnie Monkey to engage your child in the new game, or you may prefer to devise your own story to illustrate the swinging, bending and rolling exercises, improvising as you go along. This sequence focuses on the arms, shoulders and spine, beginning with some easy gymnastics and moving on to simple acrobatics that also strengthen and relax the entire body. Start gradually, allowing your child to become accustomed to each new movement before progressing to the next.

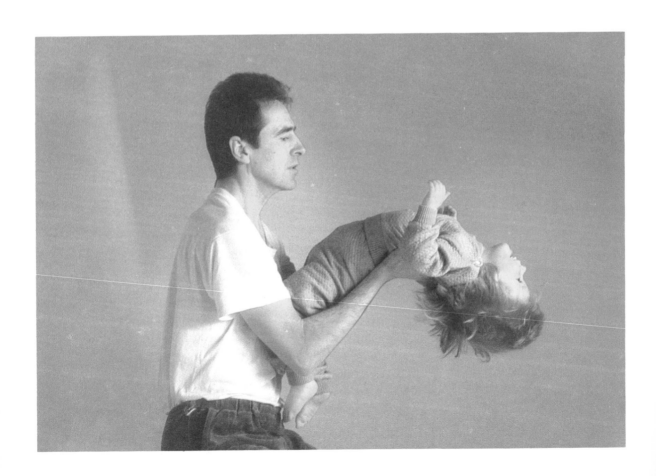

Swings, somersaults and bends

The following sequence of soft gymnastics promotes relaxed strength and flexibility throughout the body, especially in the arms, shoulders, back and spine. Go through the sequence slowly, and for safety and comfort use a soft surface, such as a duvet, and ensure that you are both barefoot. Read your child's instructions out loud.

1 ♂ Kneel comfortably on the floor, facing your child.
☆ Tell your child: "Bend over and put your hands and head on the floor, like Olga Ostrich. Keep your legs straight."

2 ♂ Help your child into a headstand, supporting the hips.
☆ "Push your feet off the floor and stand on your head."

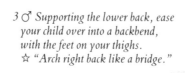

3 ♂ Supporting the lower back, ease your child over into a backbend, with the feet on your thighs.
☆ "Arch right back like a bridge."

4 ♂ Still supporting the lower back, open your knees and let the child's feet touch the floor for an instant. Then immediately help your child to stand up, keeping one hand under the lower back and the other under the upper back.
☆ "Bend back further and put your toes on the floor, then your feet. Now stand up."

5 ♂ Stand facing your child and hold the forearms. Bend your knees and let your child step on to your knees.
☆ "Step up on to my knees."

6 ♂ Keep a firm grip as your child walks up to your waist.
☆ "Walk right up to my waist."

7 ♂ Still holding tight, allow your child to tip upside-down, so that your thighs support the back.
☆ "Now turn right upside-down."

8 ♂ Allow your child to roll over.
☆ "Push off with your feet and roll right the way over, so that everything turns right around."

9 ♂ As your child rolls, bend your
knees and lean forward, so that the
feet reach the floor easily.
☆ "Bring your feet to the floor."

10 ♂ As your child comes back on to
two feet, bend slightly and swing his
or her arms down and back round to
the front.
☆ "Now stand up straight again."

11 ♂ Stand behind your child and,
holding the hands and forearms, lift
and swing from side to side two or
three times. Then rest.

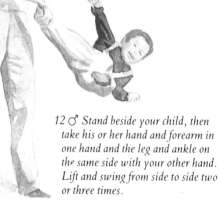

12 ♂ Stand beside your child, then
take his or her hand and forearm in
one hand and the leg and ankle on
the same side with your other hand.
Lift and swing from side to side two
or three times.

Caution:
Always hold your child's
forearms, not just the hands, and
never swing for long without
resting.

8
LEARNING TO SWIM

Swimming is a universal recreation, a source of enormous pleasure enjoyed by children and adults of all ages, cultures, and dispositions. Teaching your child to swim is an important aspect of childcare that not only opens up a new area of play and exploration, but also gives your child vital protection in and around water.

Babies take naturally to water, having spent the first nine months of life in a liquid environment. For the first few months after birth, young babies often instinctively hold their breath and make reflex "swimming" movements, if immersed in water. From the very beginning, however, it is a good idea to cultivate your child's confidence in the water and his or her trust in your support. From bathing with your baby to teaching your child to swim, time spent together in the water can become a pleasure to be anticipated with mutual enjoyment.

As long as your child learns to swim, the precise age at which he or she begins is not important. In very young babies, however, the circulation and immune systems are not fully developed. For this reason, it is important that your baby is protected against water-borne infections and that the pool is the correct temperature. It would be wise to check with your doctor and the swimming pool before your first visit.

If introduced to the pool within the first year, many children can learn to swim unaided by about three, but all children progress at their own pace and some swim earlier, some later. While your child is learning to swim, you will both feel more at ease if, maintaining the trust and confidence you have already established, you avoid over-zealousness and allow your child's pleasure to guide you. Swimming is one of the best all-round forms of exercise, strengthening the heart and lungs, improving circulation and respiration and stimulating the appetite. It makes the body feel weightless, encourages movement in all directions, and improves general strength and flexibility. With the emphasis on regular practice, patience and affection, your child will delight in and benefit from learning to swim.

This chapter includes: relaxation with your baby in the bath; an introduction to floating, fun and relaxation on a first visit to the pool; a routine of well-constructed playful techniques that cultivate water confidence and encourage your child to learn to swim and feel at ease in the water; and resuscitation techniques for emergencies.

BATHING TOGETHER

Getting used to water at home

Bathtime offers a natural opportunity to introduce your baby to the water. Within the safe confines of the bath, you can learn to handle your baby with confidence, so that he or she begins to trust you and to relax in water. Bathing together can be great fun and by introducing a little constructive play, you can encourage your infant to explore physical movements in water, as a prelude to swimming. Above all, however, bathtime should be a pleasure. Be sure to play in soap-free water and to wash your baby at the end of bathtime, taking care to shield the eyes from soap or shampoo. It is also a good idea to end bathtime before your baby gets bored. If, for some reason, your baby shows signs of fear or distress, an occasional feed given in the bath may help him or her to re-associate water with pleasure.

1 Check that the bath water is at body temperature, then get in with your baby. If the baby shows signs of distress, keep him or her in an upright position and, talking soothingly, hold your baby close and try a feed.

2 When you are both comfortable in
the water, sit your baby facing you,
supported on your thighs. Sing and
talk as you bounce and rock the baby
very gently from side to side.

3 Now lower your knees and,
supporting the back of your baby's
head with one hand and the base of
the spine with the other, allow the
baby to float.

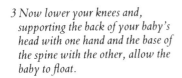

4 Turn your baby round and,
supporting the back of the head and
neck on your shoulder and both sides
of the spine with your forearms,
gently paddle the baby's legs in the
water with plenty of splashing.

AT THE POOL
The first visit

On your first visit to the pool, check that the water temperature is around 86°F (30°C). Dress your baby in towelling pants, rather than plastic knickers. Spend a few minutes walking around with your baby, allowing him or her to adjust to the echoing sounds and the wide expanse of water. Putting safety first, take your time getting into the water and dip your baby in little by little. When the water is shoulder-high on you both, let your baby get used to the smell of chlorine. Splash around a little, and bounce the baby gently in and out of the water. When you feel your baby is ready, but not before, start with a little floating. If he or she is unhappy, go back a few steps and start again, more slowly. Always give your baby your fullest attention, and be sure to maintain eye contact. Leave while he or she still wants more, limiting each session to around 20 minutes. After each swim, feed your baby, and rinse off the chlorine.

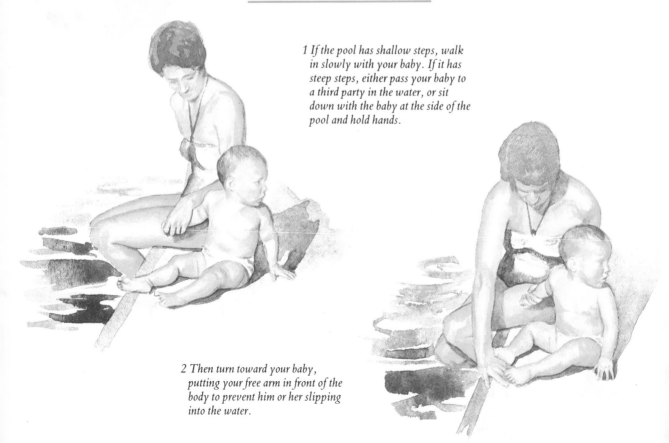

1 If the pool has shallow steps, walk in slowly with your baby. If it has steep steps, either pass your baby to a third party in the water, or sit down with the baby at the side of the pool and hold hands.

2 Then turn toward your baby, putting your free arm in front of the body to prevent him or her slipping into the water.

3 Lower yourself carefully into the water, then lift your baby off the side of the pool and into your arms.

4 Cuddle your baby and give him or her time to get used to the temperature and smell of the water. Then, talking reassuringly, gradually lower the baby into the water with you. Gently bounce up and down and sway from side to side, still talking affectionately.

5 As your baby begins to feel at ease, dip further into the water, until you are both neck-high. Then encourage your baby to blow bubbles.

SWIMMING TECHNIQUES

A safe introduction to swimming

Being able to swim can save your life. Sooner or later your child will spend time in or around water – at the sea, by a river, lake, or swimming pool. If your child can swim, the experience will be much more fun for him or her and far less nerve-racking for you. Remember, however, never to leave a young child unsupervised around water. The following techniques have the approval of the Amateur Swimming Association and are currently taught by professional instructors to give babies and children confidence in the water. When practised regularly and with enjoyment, these techniques are immensely effective. Your approach, however, is equally important. If you treat each stage as an affectionate game, allow the child's pleasurable responses to guide you, and avoid pushing beyond your child's limits, you will find he or she delights in this new achievement.

Ready steady go

Once babies are used to going underwater, they become more confident and are less likely to gasp for air and swallow water when splashed or submerged accidentally. Introduce this sequence gradually, one at a time.

1 To indicate that something special is about to happen, say: "ready, steady, go." Look into your baby's eyes and on the word "go", lift him or her high into the air then down immediately.

2 Bring your baby down into the water, letting the water splash down over the shoulders. Repeat this a few times, and on each visit, bring your baby further down into the pool until the water comes up to chin level, then to just below the nostrils.

3 Once your baby is happy to be submerged up to the nose, repeat: "ready, steady, go." Make eye contact, and lift your baby up into the air then down into the water. Allow the head to submerge fully before lifting the baby out of the water again immediately.

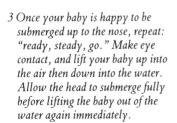

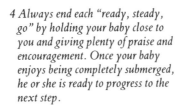

4 Always end each "ready, steady, go" by holding your baby close to you and giving plenty of praise and encouragement. Once your baby enjoys being completely submerged, he or she is ready to progress to the next step.

Learning to float

When your baby is confident
enough to relax in the water
without lifting the head or limbs,
he or she will soon be able to float
unaided. Practise each exercise for
two or three sessions before
progressing to the next, and help
your baby to enjoy each one.

*1 Babies under six months old enjoy
floating with the minimum of
support – one hand under the head
and one under the base of the spine.
You may even find that one hand
under the head is enough.*

*2 From about six months on, your
baby may resist. If so, you could try
supporting his or her head on your
shoulder, with your arms and hands
supporting the entire back, until
water confidence returns.*

*3 When you feel your baby is relaxed
and confident, gradually withdraw
your support, just keeping one hand
at the base of the head. Finally,
when appropriate, release your
hand, and be ready to lift your baby
when necessary.*

Building up to swimming

The following sequence is designed to reinforce the patterns of movement needed to swim – kicking, stretching the arms, and supporting the body horizontally in the water – while increasing your baby's confidence in the water. Practise each exercise as an affectionate game and repeat as often as your baby allows.

1 Support your baby horizontally in the water with your hands under the upper chest and the heels of your hands under the chin. Walk slowly backward, moving your baby very gently through the water.

2 Support your baby face forward on your shoulder, and hold one leg in each hand. Move your baby gently through the water, repeating: "kick, kick" as you help the legs to kick.

3 Now withdraw your hands from the legs, hold your baby's upper arms and move gently backward through the water, encouraging your baby to remain horizontal and to kick.

4 Once your baby can kick in the water, playtime can include these exercises using waterwings or floats.

Bathtime is an excellent introduction to the water and feeding your baby in the bath will help to make it a happy experience.

Most children love a piggyback in the water – it gives them the sensation of a relaxed swimming stroke.

Learning to float gives children added confidence in the water, while relaxing the body and mind.

Holding on to the side and kicking helps the child to strengthen his or her legs and to stay horizontal in the water.

5 *Supporting each side of the chest, hold your baby in front of you, so that the head is above water level. Move gently across the pool, pushing a toy out in front, so that the baby continually stretches his or her arms to reach for it.*

6 *Now face your baby, and hold the forearms. Walk slowly backward, gently pulling him or her through the water. Encourage your baby to keep the arms straight and the body horizontal.*

7 *Whenever your baby plays with a float, encourage him or her to straighten both arms.*

8 To reinforce the pattern of arm movements, practise straight-arm exercises with your child, extending one arm at a time as you move through the water.

9 When the arm and leg movements are established, encourage your baby to swim between yourself and your partner. At first be sure that one of you receives the baby as soon as the other lets go, then gradually move apart, allowing him or her to swim two or three strokes between you.

10 Increase the distance between yourself and your partner or encourage your baby to swim to the side, from increasing distances.

Once relaxed in the water, children soon progress from "baby paddle" to more advanced swimming strokes.

It will take a little practice to develop a strong kick and straight arms and legs.

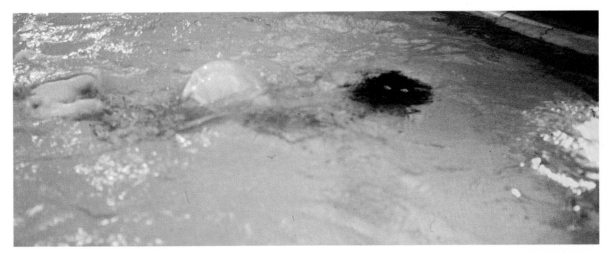

1 Having learned to swim on the surface, many children long to explore underwater. Remind your child to take a deep breath.

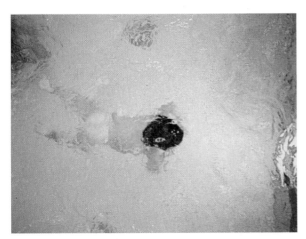

2 Encourage the child to aim for a focal point, such as a light, not too far away.

3 Once submerged, the child will instinctively stretch toward the light.

4 It will take some strong thrusts to stay underwater.

5 Stay close as your child reaches the light and rises to the surface.

Jumping in and getting out

For children who love the water, jumping in holds a magnetic attraction. But any child may be pushed or fall in, so whether your child naturally wants to jump in or not, it makes good sense to teach him or her how to jump into water and how to get out again safely afterward.

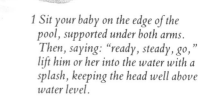

1 Sit your baby on the edge of the pool, supported under both arms. Then, saying: "ready, steady, go," lift him or her into the water with a splash, keeping the head well above water level.

2 When your baby has gained confidence, stand him or her on the edge of the pool. Hold both hands and, without supporting the weight, encourage the baby to jump in and go under briefly before lifting him or her out again immediately.

3 The next stage is to encourage your child to jump into your arms from the side of the pool. As you catch the child, bring your arms down to allow him or her to submerge before lifting up again immediately.

4 You can now encourage your child to jump in alone. Allow him or her to go under, then lift the head and shoulders from the water immediately.

5 To find out which direction your child naturally turns in the water, call him or her from behind. Get into the water and let your child jump in. This time, as you lift the head and shoulders from the water, turn your child in the preferred direction back to the side of the pool.

Caution:
Babies and young children should always have constant supervision around water.

6 Having taught your child how to jump in, now help him or her to get out. Encourage your child to lift one leg on to the rail and pull him- or herself up over the edge, as you give a little push on the buttocks.

Resuscitation and cardiac massage

Every second counts if there is an accident, so act immediately. Remove any obvious obstruction from the child's mouth, but don't waste time trying to clear any unseen congestion in the throat. Try to get air into the lungs immediately, as shown below, making sure that the tongue is not sagging into the throat to block the air passage. If this happens, push the chin upward. If the abdomen rises, air is reaching the stomach instead of the lungs, so pull the jaw further forward and arch the neck more. After immediate resuscitation, always take the child to hospital for treatment. In the event of a fall or dive into shallow water, always assume that there may be a neck or back injury and do not bend or turn the neck. Never leave young children, even swimmers, alone near water.

Resuscitating a child (over 2)

Seal your lips around the child's nose and mouth, relax, and blow gently about 15 times a minute. The child may start breathing immediately, but it can take several minutes or sometimes even hours, so don't give up while there is a chance that the child may revive. (See recovery position, right.)

Resuscitating a baby (under 2)

Seal your lips around the baby's nose and mouth, relax, and blow gently about 20 times a minute. Give the first four puffs in quick succession and then blow rhythmically every three seconds. After a while listen for an exhalation. If you don't hear it, give four quick puffs and carry on. Persist until the baby starts to breathe independently. (See recovery position, right.)

Cardiac massage

If there is no sign of a heartbeat, lay the child flat on his or her back on a firm surface and combine external heart massage with mouth-to-mouth resuscitation. Ideally two people should perform this – one giving heart massage, the other giving mouth-to-mouth. This technique is best learned from an expert.

Cardiac massage for a baby

With a baby, press two fingers of one hand rhythmically and firmly against the bottom of the breast bone, a hundred times a minute.

Caution:

Never perform heart massage when there is the slightest evidence of a pulse.

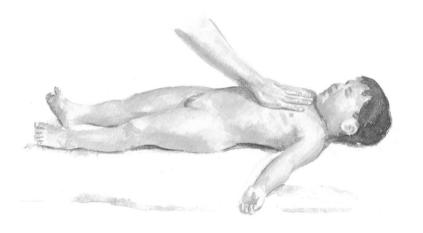

Cardiac massage for a child

With a child, press the heel of your hand firmly and rhythmically against the bottom of the breast bone, a hundred times a minute.

Recovery position

Once the baby or child is breathing, lay him or her on one side, cover with a blanket, and seek prompt medical attention. Continue to watch carefully, in case further resuscitation is necessary.

BODY MAP

Skeleton and muscles

The skeleton is a living bony framework that supports and protects the vulnerable organs and soft tissues of the body. The bones of the skeleton are bound to each other at their joints by ligaments, and are pulled into movement by the muscles, which are also attached to the bones. The muscles act upon the bones in pairs of mutual opposites, so that as one muscle contracts to pull the bone into action, the other relaxes and stretches as shown below. Tension and bad posture can tire the muscles by forcing them to contract constantly. Stretching helps to counteract this effect, leaving the muscles and ligaments more relaxed and the joints more mobile. Stretching exercises are also helpful in pregnancy when the weight of the baby places increasing strain on the postural muscles.

When the biceps (on the front of the upper arm) contracts, it shortens and pulls the forearm up.

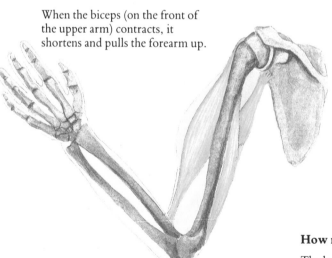

The triceps relaxes and stretches to allow the biceps to contract and the forearm to move.

How muscles work

The bones of the skeleton are bound together at their joints by tough, fibrous ligaments. The muscles attached to the bones function in pairs. When one tightens and contracts to move the bone, the other relaxes and stretches to allow the movement. Regular exercise ensures that the muscles contract and relax with ease to allow a wide range of movement.

Bones, muscles and joints

The muscles and joints together constitute some ¾ of the body's total mass and weight. An increase in their efficiency, through exercise, can help to improve the body's shape and the working of its internal systems.

The spine is the body's central pillar of support and is held upright chiefly by the muscles in the back. Tight abdominal muscles can pull the chest and shoulders forward and so undermine the integrity of the spinal column, giving rise to back-ache.

The head is held in balance on the top of the spinal column by the pull of the muscles on the sides of the neck. Stiff neck muscles can transmit tension from the top of the shoulders and the back of the neck across the top of the head, causing headaches.

The flexibility of the hip joints is crucial to the strength and integrity of the back. Stiff hips cause unbalanced standing and sitting postures, which eventually result in back pain.

If the calf muscles and the backs of the thighs are supple, the body can bend easily from the hip joints and sit more comfortably, with the weight on the backs of the legs, instead of on the back of the buttocks.

The legs are the body's roots and any stiffness that impedes the functioning of their muscles and joints can affect the structural symmetry of the entire body.

The even development of the strength and suppleness of the postural muscles, and the flexibility of the knees and ankles, allow the body to move with greater ease and mobility.

INDEX

Recommended reading

Hugh Jolly *Book of Child Care* George Allen & Unwin 1985. Janet Balaskas *The Active Birth Partners Handbook* Sidgwick & Jackson 1984. Dr Thomas Verney with John Kelly *The Secret Life of the Unborn Child* Sphere Books 1982. Aiden Macfarlane *The Psychology of Childbirth* Fontana 1977. Peter Walker *Baby Relax* George Allen and Unwin 1986. Arthur Balaskas and Peter Walker *Baby Gymnastics* George Allen & Unwin 1987. Maire Messenger *The Breastfeeding Book* Century Publishing 1982. Lennart Nilsson *A Child is Born* Faber & Faber. Dr Miriam Stoppard *Pregnancy & Birth Book* Dorling Kindersley 1985. Nancy Kohner *You and Your Baby* Orbis 1984.

ACKNOWLEDGEMENTS

Authors' acknowledgements

Special thanks to Janet Balaskas for her good work with parents-to-be, and to the Active Birth Centre; thanks particularly to the production team at Gaia – Rosanne, Sara, Fausto and Peter – and to Joss, Lucy and Anna for making the book possible; and many thanks to Carol A. Hicks for her time and effort and contributions toward the swimming techniques, and to Lollie Stirk, Cookie Ross, Duncan Cohen, Charles Edmondson, Betty Hoare, Alice Coyle, Jeff and Pat Davis, Barry and Sheila, David Hicks and Club Sport.

Publisher's acknowledgements

Gaia Books would like to thank the following for their invaluable help: Peter Mennim for his beautiful illustrations, Fausto Dorelli for his enticing photographs, Joss Pearson for her advice and encouragement, Lucy Lidell for all her guidance and help, Peter Warren for photographic assistance, Carol A. Hicks for her time and expert assistance, Alice Coyle, Betty Hoare and Dr Charles Edmondson for expert advice, Peter Furtado for working against time, Michael Burman, Imogen Bright, Ros Mair, Susan Walby, Lesley Gilbert, Jane Carr, David Reynolds, Alan Wherry, David Hicks at the National Sports Centre, Crystal Palace, Keith Lyons at the Elephant and Castle Sports Centre, St John's Ambulance, Ross Mackelvie and Alfa Electronics for flash equipment, and On Yer Bike.

Photographic models

Peter, Fiona, Jason and Mimi Cookie Ross
Mark Christie
Teruko Chagrin and baby Alyusha Mamiko
Christina and Murray Lovett and baby Alex
Michelle Brown and Ian Diggs and baby Stevie
Clare and Bridget Nugent
Jackie Stephens and Sandie Roots
Judy Miller and baby Otis
Duncan Cohen
Helen Rowson and baby Alfie.

Photographic credits

All photographs were taken by Fausto Dorelli, with the following exceptions:
Pp.14, 18-19, 22-23 by Lennart Nilsson; p.48 by Vision International/Anthea Sieveking.